"Let Kala Ambrose be your tour guide to t̶ T0153133
revenants of New Orleans. What so distingu̶i̶s̶h̶e̶s̶ ̶t̶h̶i̶s̶ ̶b̶o̶o̶k̶ ̶f̶r̶o̶m̶
the rest of the contenders is the respect with which Ambrose treats
spiritual topics—something that is indeed rare. She writes about
New Orleans with love, offering practical travel advice alongside
chilling tales of ghosts and vampires. Highly recommended!"

—Judika Illes, author of *Encyclopedia of 5,000 Spells;*
Encyclopedia of Spirits; and
Encyclopedia of Mystics, Saints & Sages

"New Orleans, a city with an almost palpable mystique of the
supernatural, the unknown, the unexplained. Imagine visiting
this iconic city with a trusted guide who can not only inform
about the extensive ethereal population of ghosts earthbound
in their old haunts, but one who also can actually speak to the
spirits themselves and relay their fascinating stories. Spiritual
teacher, priestess, and oracle Kala Ambrose has written a fascinating book that is bound to become a paranormal classic."

—Brad Steiger, author of
Real Ghosts, Restless Spirits, and Haunted Places

"Kala Ambrose's *Spirits of New Orleans* shows us how New
Orleans is a magical city filled with hidden spiritual secrets—it
is a practical, entertaining, and expert guide to its other side."

—Bradford P. Keeney, Ph.D. & Hillary Keeney, Ph.D.,
authors, professors, and internationally renowned spiritual
teachers; The Mojo Doctors, New Orleans

"Once again, Kala Ambrose delivers the supernatural goods
and takes us on a wild ride as we discover the truth about the
paranormal entities of one of the nation's most mysterious of all
places: New Orleans."

—Nick Redfern, author of *Monster Diary*

Titles in the *America's Haunted Road Trip* Series:

SPIRITS OF NEW ORLEANS

Voodoo Curses, Vampire Legends, and Cities of the Dead

KALA AMBROSE

CLERISY PRESS

Dedicated to the people of New Orleans—
past, present, and future . . .

Spirits of New Orleans: Voodoo Curses, Vampire Legends, and Cities of the Dead

For further information, contact the publisher at:
Clerisy Press
An imprint of AdventureKEEN
306 Greenup Street
Covington, KY 41011
www.clerisypress.com

Library of Congress Cataloging-in-Publication Data

Ambrose, Kala, 1966–
  Spirits of New Orleans : voodoo curses, vampire legends, and the cities of the dead / by Kala Ambrose. — First edition.
    pages cm — (America's haunted road trip)
  ISBN 978-1-57860-509-5 (pbk.) — ISBN 1-57860-509-1 (pbk.)
  ISBN 978-1-57860-510-1 (ebook) — ISBN 978-1-57860-623-8 (hardcover)
  1. Ghosts—Louisiana—New Orleans. 2. Haunted places—Louisiana—New Orleans. I. Title.

  BF1472.U6A457 2012
  133.109763'35--dc23

                                    2012018953

Distributed by Publishers Group West
Printed in the United States of America
First edition, first printing

Editor: Vanessa Rusch Thomas
Cover design: Scott McGrew
Cover and interior photos provided by the author unless otherwise noted

TABLE OF CONTENTS

Introduction

Embracing the Spirit and Spirits of New Orleans

> *"Seeing a ghost in New Orleans is as common as having a bowl of gumbo. The question is not when but where best to savor them both. Each person who lives or visits the city of New Orleans quickly finds his or her favorite haunts and returns to them time and time again."*
>
> —Kala Ambrose

AS AN INTUITIVE CHILD growing up in Louisiana, my soul flourished along the running waters of the Mississippi Delta, the Red River, and the Gulf Coast. I grew up seeing ghosts, as well as hearing about the haunted history of each location we visited. While most every city in Louisiana has its haunted tales, my favorite has always been New Orleans.

New Orleans is a port city known for its food, where a thick roux base is mixed with spices, vegetables, seafood, meat, and everything else in the kitchen, and is thrown into a gumbo pot to the culinary satisfaction of the most discerning soul. This unique, eclectic mixture spills over into the people and their history, creating—among other things—some of the most soulful and haunting music the world has ever seen. The spirit of New Orleans is so enticing that whenever I hear blues or jazz music playing, I have to stop what I'm doing and dance to the rhythm reaching deep within my soul, connecting me to the roots of my mind, body, and spirit.

Present-day New Orleans on Bourbon Street

The energy of this land is so potent and powerful that it places a hold on each person who enters these swampy grounds and claims you as its own. This may explain in part why the city of New Orleans is so haunted with ghosts much older than its current residents.

One never runs out of things to experience in NOLA (New Orleans, Louisiana). Recently, I returned to my roots in the great state of Louisiana and spent some time in my favorite place in the world: the French Quarter of New Orleans. Truly captivating, this city is a veritable feast for all five senses, as well as the sixth sense.

The best way to describe how I feel in this city is charmed. New Orleans is many things to many people, but for me it is charming and embodies a spirit—a joy for living (joie de vivre)—that is expressed throughout the city.

I remember the first time I returned to New Orleans after Hurricane Katrina. I had no idea how the vibe of the city would feel after having gone through such a horrific experience. My heart was thrilled to see that the great lady was holding her own with a state of grace, while still undergoing major renovations on the physical, mental, emotional, and spiritual levels.

I traveled around parts of the city riding the streetcars, taking in each neighborhood, enjoying the stunning architecture, smelling honeysuckle and jasmine in the air, and chuckling at the sight of Mardi Gras beads hanging from the boughs of trees. As the streetcar delivered me near the French Market, the smell of beignets and coffee coming from Café du Monde lifted my spirit. Yes, I sighed with relief; New Orleans has been through the worst and still she stands—proud, strong, and vibrant.

It is my sincere belief that New Orleans is charmed: charmed by the artists and musicians when their art and music spill into the streets touching the soul at the core, charmed by the chefs who tantalize our appetites in sweet rhapsody with their culinary delights, and charmed by the people who are kind, good natured, and some of the most loving and joyful people who I have ever had the pleasure of knowing.

THE JOURNEY BEGINS

As we begin this journey into the spirit and spirits of New Orleans, we will tread carefully into the cities of the dead and visit the land of magical Voodoo queens. Growing up in Louisiana, I assumed that people everywhere spoke about mojo, gris-gris, juju, and Voodoo and celebrated Mardi Gras and other joyous occasions, for the simple joy of being alive and around family and friends. Later, as I lived and traveled around the country, I soon discovered that Louisiana has a very unique style of living. There is no other place like it in the world. I'm of French, Scottish, Irish, and German origin, and my family has lived in almost every area of the state. My mother was a Cajun queen born in Lafayette; my great-grandmother lived in South Louisiana, where she supported her family by reading tea leaves and making folk remedies.

I grew up attending Mardi Gras in New Orleans, where I was carried through the city on my father's broad shoulders, free to stretch out my hands and catch beads as the floats passed by. He tirelessly carried me through these parades, carrying bags of beads, doubloons, and other items that I collected. At the age of 3, at a game with my parents, I first danced to the LSU fight song during halftime, to the delight of family and spectators, who remarked that even at this early age I had the rhythm and spirit of Louisiana in my soul. I was raised Catholic; went to school where I was taught by nuns; played along the Red River; went crabbing, fishing, and inner tubing; and grew up in a state where people celebrated the joy in everyday life. I can't really remember a weekend growing up when my parents weren't having a party of some kind, with family and friends dropping by and a huge variety of food being cooked and shared by everyone. Everyone I met was an honorary uncle or aunt, and no one stayed a stranger for long.

I also grew up having psychic abilities, as well as the ability to see ghosts and communicate with the spirit world. I began having prophetic dreams at an early age and began communicating with beings that I first attributed to being my guardian angels. I spent the majority of my free time in the libraries getting my hands on every book I could find on the subjects of ancient mythology, ancient history, the ancient gods of Egypt, the oracles of Greece, Celtic traditions, comparative world history and religions, and ancient spiritual practices. I also loved to read ghost stories and legends. This passion for all of these topics began at the age of 5 or 6, and I have never looked back.

Author Kala Ambrose in New Orleans

As my psychic abilities grew and developed, it did not take me long to realize that I had been born into a magical land. Louisiana is a land where magic still lives, a place where time stands still in a primordial fashion, and portals in the swamplands open to the supernatural realms where fairies and other mystical creatures roam.

It is a land so ancient and powerful that the magic is still afoot. With a simple call to action, this energy rises from the fertile rich soil of the Mississippi Delta and the Gulf Coast and awakens to answer your call. I grew up with a healthy respect for this magic and with the understanding that this magic also lives within me.

I heard the siren song of the muses who stand guard over Louisiana, and I answered their call very early in life. Though I have traveled and lived in many areas of the United States, I have always held the spirit of Louisiana in my heart and soul. She and I are one, and her magic runs deep into my core. Each time I return, the ancient magic stirs and recognizes that this is my home. Each day that I stay in New Orleans, deeper memories of past lives spent here in the city surface. Each time I write about New Orleans, the people and their ghosts join me in remembrance of times gone by in the hope that New Orleans is to be reborn once again.

Join me on this magical mystery tour as I become your travel guide to the other side. As your travel guide, I'll point out the history, mystery, and legends of the city that you may have passed by before without knowing what lay in wait inside. I'll also share with you which ghosts are still actively haunting the city and why. By the end of this journey, you may also find yourself enchanted and charmed by the spirit of Louisiana and New Orleans.

For those of you who have never been to the city, I'm going to introduce you to the lady and beguile you into falling in love with her. For those of you have been to NOLA and haven't been back in awhile, I'm going to help you fall in love all over again.

In this book we will explore the history of the city and those who decided to make it their eternal home, as a resting place for some and a point of revenge for others. As the legendary Bette Davis once said, "Fasten your seat belts—it's going to be a bumpy night," as we delve into Voodoo curses, vampire legends, lost souls, and the cities of the dead.

Once the romance of the city is fully in bloom, I'll be your guide into the dark side of the city, where ghosts haunt the streets and every corner. I'll show you where I've run into ghosts and other supernatural entities in broad daylight and on foggy nights, and I'll share with you some of the most haunted sites in the city.

At the end of this ride, you'll come away knowing a great deal about the history of New Orleans and her people, as well as the ghosts who have decided they will never leave.

New Orleans—Past, Present, and Future

The city has been in the news lately regarding politics, disaster recovery efforts (and non-efforts), crime, and, most recently, the Gulf of Mexico oil spill. Each report is extremely important and is of great concern.

I often worry some days about the coming earth changes and if cities such as New Orleans will one day be swallowed up by the oceans and remain only a distant memory. Perhaps we will tell future generations about the city that had such a generosity of spirit that it threw the world's biggest free party and Carnival every year for all who wished to attend. Magnificent floats were built, people wore elaborate costumes, and everyone danced in the streets wearing boas and catching the free souvenirs, such as beads and doubloons, being tossed to them.

I think about this and wonder if these future generations shake their heads in disbelief while living in cold steel cities where parades consist of little more than uniform marching bands with small banners. Perhaps they'll laugh at these tales and compare them to the mythological stories of the cities Atlantis and Lemuria.

For this reason, I write in the hopes that future generations will know that true magical cities did and do exist, and, if at all possible, those who can will move heaven and earth to see that New Orleans survives. Her soul belongs to the muses and the bohemians who heed the call of art, music, literature, dance, theater, history, self-expression, and love in all forms.

New Orleans is a unique and deeply important part of the United States that must be preserved. In many ways, it is the soul of this great land, where music, art, and creative enterprises are born and venture onward throughout the country on the wings of muses to the delight and joy of many.

My intent here is to share the beauty and the magic of New Orleans in harmony with the haunted history in a city so special and so unique that it truly deserves to be respected as a rich cultural treasure.

The stories and information I share here are true to the best of my knowledge, experience, and research. History is never truly accurate in all accounts, and many of these stories have been passed down orally through the generations. As such, the possibility of some of the information being embellished and changed over time may have occurred. The story of the LaLaurie house is one example where recent further research revealed a completely new twist to the haunted tale. In due diligence, I've collected eyewitness accounts, local lore and legends, and stories based on these beautiful haunted spaces. I then attempted to confirm as many of these details as possible by court records, museums, and other legal documents and books available regarding these stories. Finally, I visited each location independently as a psychic and a medium to see what I could discern and experience in each location and, when possible, to speak with the spirits directly.

The result of this investigation is presented here in the *Spirits of New Orleans*. May the tales of these spirits delight, entertain, and enchant you along the journey.

In love, joy, and a sprinkle of magic,
~Kala~

 Kala's Travel Tips

To enjoy the music and spirit of New Orleans, listen to **WWOZ Radio 90.7FM,** the New Orleans Jazz and Heritage Station. When not in the city, you can still listen to the station streaming online at wwoz.org or from your smart phone with its app.

CHAPTER 1

The Grande Dame City of the Dead—St. Louis Cemetery #1

"The first thing you notice about New Orleans are the bury-ing grounds—the cemeteries—and they're a cold proposi-tion, one of the best things there are here. Going by, you try to be as quiet as possible, better to let them sleep. Greek, Roman, sepulchres—palatial mausoleums made to order, phantomesque, signs and symbols of hidden decay—ghosts of women and men who have sinned and who've died and are now living in tombs. The past doesn't pass away so quickly here. You could be dead for a long time."

—Bob Dylan, *Chronicles: Volume One*

OF ALL OF THE CITIES IN THE WORLD to be buried, New Orleans is always my first choice.

The art of dying has been refined to an art form in NOLA. The legendary jazz funerals are the most distinguished, elo-quent, and touching rituals juxtaposed against modern-day living as a fitting send-off to the spirit world. Based on a com-bination of African and European traditions, a jazz funeral begins with a processional march of the deceased's family, friends, and a brass band, which leads the way from the funeral home to the cemetery.

As the music attracts the attention of passersby and neigh-bors, people recognize what is occurring and often join the group in the march in what is described as the second line. The first line is the official group that received a parade per-mit or, in this case, a permit for the funeral march. The second

Pathway through St. Louis Cemetery #1

line is comprised of people who hear the call and lure of the music and spontaneously join in to participate in the celebration or to be a part of the final send-off for the deceased. Second-line participants often carry colorful parasols and wave handker-chiefs in the air while dancing down the street. The dances are organic, free, and a celebrated art form.

The music is somber on the journey to the cemetery, por-traying the grief and loss experienced by those left behind. Once the deceased has been laid to rest, the procession marches on to the place designated for everyone to gather together. Along this march, the music picks up in tempo and becomes lively, both as a celebration of the life of the person laid to rest and to symbolize that life goes on. Most people begin to dance with abandon, and the emotional release is powerful and palatable and spreads throughout the group in the streets. Some of the most recognized songs played are "Just a Closer Walk with Thee" and "When the Saints Go Marching In." It is one of the most stirring, intimate, loving, joyful, and heartfelt experiences one can observe, and I can think of no finer way to be laid to rest.

ENTER THE CITIES OF THE DEAD

Once the deceased has been carried soulfully through the procession, they are laid to rest in cemeteries, which, in New Orleans, are described as the cities of the dead.

St. Louis Cemetery #1, founded in 1789, is one of the most famous cemeteries in the country. Located on the corner of St. Louis and Basin Streets about a block away from the French Quarter, the cemetery is so distinctive that it's nearly impossible to miss. The reason is that in New Orleans, the cemeteries are filled with so many aboveground tombs that they look like small cities rather than the expansive lawns with small stones and crosses that people are more familiar with in other parts of the country. The cemeteries—with their tiny buildings located so close together—look like a miniature-sized city, which has earned them the nickname the cities of the dead.

There are actually three St. Louis Cemeteries in New Orleans, named respectively #1, #2, and #3, but St. Louis Cemetery #1 is the one that receives the greatest attention. St. Louis Cemetery #2 is several blocks away from #1 and is much larger in size— roughly three square blocks compared to the one-block size of #1. St. Louis Cemetery #2 is the final resting place of many talented and legendary jazz and rhythm and blues musicians, including one of my favorites, Ernie K. Doe. It is also the resting place of Henriette Delille, the founder of the Sisters of the Holy Family, who is currently being considered for sainthood by the Catholic church. Farthest away from the French Quarter is St. Louis Cemetery #3, located near Bayou St. John, which has some of the most beautiful and elaborate tombs of all.

Many people who visit New Orleans are surprised to discover that the crescent-shaped city is actually below sea level, which is what led to aboveground burials in tombs. One of the most interesting places to view this anomaly is near Café du Monde across from Jackson Square, where you can walk up a flight of steps on the levee to see the Mississippi River above the area. There's something very eerie the first time you do this, as you have the feeling of standing on the edge of a very full bowl of water and realizing that, with one big splash, the water could come spilling over. Indeed this is what occurred when the levees failed in the lower Ninth Ward, causing the area to flood after Hurricane Katrina.

Interestingly, though, when sitting at Café du Monde enjoying some beignets (fried doughnuts covered in mounds of powdered sugar) and French coffee while listening to musicians performing live on the streets, the slightly disturbing situation of the water looming above nearby escapes your thoughts, and you find yourself swirling back into the energy and falling in love with New Orleans.

Be that as it may, New Orleans is still under sea level and slowly descending further at a rate of a quarter inch each year. Built on swampy wet grounds, early settlers soon discovered that it was impossible to bury the dead underground, for as soon as a good rain came through, the buried caskets would float up to the top and sometimes even shoot out of the ground, to the shock and unsettling grief of family and friends. Even more gruesome, over time some of the wooden caskets would break apart underground, which allowed decaying body parts and bones to float up to the surface and down the streets as they were carried away by the water. Several attempts were made over the years to find a way to keep the caskets underground—including boring holes in the bottom of the caskets so that the water could enter the casket and flow through the holes into the ground—along with attempts to weigh the caskets down to make them heavier. However, neither idea worked, and the dead continued to rise when floodwaters and heavy rains came through. It was as if the dead wanted to be considered and not forgotten as a part of New Orleans, even long after they had left their mortal coil.

After several particularly heavy storms where the dead floated down the streets, the decision was made to establish a system of vaults and aboveground tombs where the dead would be laid to rest in peace. While many attribute flooding as the only reason that the wall vaults and tombs were built, some historians and scholars believe that this was only part of the decision for this design. As New Orleans grew as a city with a wealthier population, many of the settlers from France and Spain desired to offer tribute to their dead in the customs from their countries, which included burying them in the European style of aboveground vaults and tombs of this design.

St. Louis Cemetery #1 covers the expanse of only one city block, yet thousands of people are buried in this cemetery. If you do the math, you'll see that no matter how close the tombs are, it would be very difficult to have this many people buried here on this land without the aboveground tombs reaching skyscraper status in height—which they do not. How then are so many people buried in such a small area? The answer lies within each tomb. Tombs, unlike gravesites, are designed to hold multiple people rather than one individual. Most of the tombs at St. Louis were created to house generations of a family. In other cases, what are known as society tombs were built and designed by members of a group, which established a designated number of wall vaults where members are buried together, and the membership continues to maintain and care for the tomb in perpetuity. Some of these society tombs are among the most striking and distinctive in the cemeteries. My favorite style is the sarcophagus tombs, which have a front entrance area and

**Marie Laveau's tomb
marked with x's**

tend to be surrounded by wrought iron gates, giving the impression of a grand home. The simplest design found in these cemeteries are the step vaults, which are blocks of stone not much larger than the size of a casket that are raised above ground in a rectangular shape. Step vaults have largely fallen out of favor, as they tend to break apart and do not hold up well against the elements. In addition, they allow for only one person to be buried in this manner, versus the other vaults and tombs, which allow for multiple generations.

With the idea in mind that generations of family or friends would be buried in these tombs, the dead were buried in wood coffins that would biodegrade over time. When space was needed in the tomb to bury the next person assigned to a specific vault, the tomb would be opened and the remains inside would be pushed to the back of the vault to accommodate the new resident. The only restriction was that the vault could only be opened after one year and one day from the prior burial. This congenial burial atmosphere was a common practice in Europe and provided an established area in one central location for families or groups to visit the burial sites of their loved ones.

Over the years, this led to thousands of people—including some of the city's most famous politicians, musicians, military heroes, and wealthy entrepreneurs—being buried in this one-block location. This cemetery is also thought to be the home of the most famous Voodoo practitioner in the world, Marie Laveau. Marie is reportedly buried in the Glapion family tomb, tomb #347, though some researchers disagree on this fact and believe that she is buried in St. Louis Cemetery #2. Most historians consider this to be a misunderstanding, due to another Voodoo practitioner named Marie Comtesse, who is buried in #2. The overwhelming majority of the people in the city agree that Marie Laveau is indeed buried in St. Louis Cemetery #1.

Marie Laveau, the original Voodoo queen, lived from 1794 to 1881, though her dates are often confused due to her daughter having the same name (Marie Laveau II), who continued her mother's work and legacy until her death in 1895. Marie's legacy remains so strong as the queen of Voodoo that, more than 130 years later, her tomb is the most-visited tomb in all of the cemeteries. The tomb is easily recognizable when walking through the cemetery as it is covered with x's. Though it is illegal to desecrate a tomb by writing on it in any way, hundreds of followers and fans visit her tomb every year and mark an x or three x's on the tomb, while asking for Marie to grant their wishes. They also bring gifts and offerings to the tomb and lay them on the ground nearby.

During my visits to St. Louis Cemetery #1 and Marie's tomb, I found cosmetics, dolls, coins, flowers, food, alcohol, tobacco,

Offerings left at Marie Laveau's tomb include cosmetics, flowers, and hair adornments.

costume jewelry, and candles placed in front of her tomb. It is customary to bring a gift to the spirits when asking for a favor, and each person who visits with a request brings something of this nature to leave behind. The legend states that to have Marie and the spirits grant your wish, you must stand at the tomb and knock three times to gain the attention of the spirit world. Once you have knocked, whisper your wish into the tomb and then draw three x's on the tomb.

While this sounds very precise and highly romantic, Voodoo practitioners will tell you that it is not the proper technique to use when asking for a favor from the spirits. In many ways, it is considered disrespectful, as well as the constant scraping on the walls being destructive to the tomb. It's hard to believe that Marie would want such a thing done to her tomb. She was known to be extremely generous and caring to the people of New Orleans. With this in mind, a simple request to her from the heart should be heard just as effectively in the spirit realms.

Should you visit the tomb one day and desire that your wish be heard, quietly stand near the tomb, offer your respects and gratitude, and whisper your wish into the wind, which will carry your message through the ethers. Should you desire a more distinctive and powerful Voodoo ceremony, there are Voodoo practitioners throughout New Orleans who are more than able to assist you with the ceremony or ritual that you are looking to create. If you were to observe any Voodoo practices going on in the cemetery, though, you would not find them here at Marie's tomb. Instead you might observe the gathering of redbrick dust, which is used for protecting homes. Louie Armstrong is one of the most famous people known to have gathered this brick dust when he was a boy to make money. He would enter the cemetery and scrape the crumbling red bricks into dust and then deliver the brick dust to practitioners so they could disperse it as needed to their customers.

While ghost stories abound in every square block of this city, an enormous amount of stories regard sightings of the ghost of Marie Laveau in the cemetery and on the streets. Most people whom I chatted with about Marie spoke of feeling her presence in St. Louis Cemetery #1 as a spiritual energy, similar to standing near a holy site or sacred ground. During my visit to St. Louis Cemetery #1, I felt the energy of several ghosts, but none of them materialized in full form. I also heard the sound of a small child weeping, which was very sorrowful.

The only time I saw a ghostly form in this location was outside the entrance to the cemetery shortly before sunset. I saw an elderly man wearing a hat and suit, standing quietly and looking as if he was thinking about going through the entrance. At first, his suit was so dark in color that I thought he really was a man standing there, but after a moment the color from his suit faded and then so did the rest of him. It appeared as if he was still unsure why he was at the cemetery and what he was doing there. This is often the case with many ghosts who stay near cemeteries, as they are still trying to figure out and comprehend that they have passed on.

There are many tales of ghostly activity from St. Louis Cemetery #2 where Marie Laveau II (the daughter) is reportedly buried in Square Three inside of a wall vault. While her mother appears to be resting in peace in the spirit world, some say that her daughter is not as settled and can be seen on moonlit nights walking through St. Louis Cemetery #2.

While this may be the case, St. Louis Cemetery #3 would be my choice of cemeteries to spend a night looking for paranormal activity. It has all the makings to be one of the most-haunted cemeteries in the area. Built on Esplanade Avenue, this area was used by Native Americans for thousands of years before the city of New Orleans was formed. In the 18th century, it was designated as a containment area, where people with leprosy were banished to live, which sadly then became a burial ground for the lepers. St. Louis Cemetery #3 was later built on top of where the lepers were buried.

The cemetery is located near Bayou St. John, which connects to Lake Pontchartrain and the Gulf of Mexico, forming a strong link to the mystical waters surrounding this area. Bayou St. John is the location where Marie Laveau and other practitioners performed some of the most potent and powerful Voodoo rituals, and thousands came to observe these rituals in action (many of which are still being practiced here to this day). Visitors longing to see something of this nature should check out St. John's Day, also known as Midsummer in New Orleans, where thousands congregate to perform sacred rituals along St. John's Bayou.

The spirits residing in St. Louis Cemetery #3 are in a magnificent real estate location near the bayou and City Park, with a front stage pass each year to the Jazz and Heritage Festival (which locals refer to as Jazz Fest). Forget about the dead turning in their graves—in New Orleans, they're more apt to rise and dance the second line! Perhaps this is why this cemetery is still one of the most popular and active cemeteries with hundreds of new burials each year.

From what I've observed in my years as a psychic medium and as a paranormal researcher, most ghosts don't hang out in the cemeteries. They are out haunting the places that they enjoyed "haunting" while they were alive. I find New Orleans to be no different in this respect. Most of the ghosts are enjoying the city alongside the living.

This brings us to the purpose of this book: to explore the supernatural beings that reside throughout the city of New Orleans. A great majority of them choose to stay in the Vieux Carre, also known as the French Quarter.

As your travel guide to the other side, I'd like to offer a few tips when visiting St. Louis Cemetery #1, along with any of the other cemeteries in the area.

⚜ KALA'S TRAVEL TIPS

- **Safety first.** It's best to visit the cemetery with a tour group during the day. While I find the cemetery itself very peaceful and enjoyable, there are reports of people being attacked and robbed by the living. It's easy for a person to hide among the tombs and catch someone who is there alone off guard. You don't want to end up being the newest resident of the cemetery, so be safe and travel with a tour group, as there is safety in numbers. It's also easier to get turned around and feel lost in the city of the dead. In addition, the tour groups provide an enormous amount of historical and entertaining information about the tombs. The cemetery is only open during the day, but some paranormal researchers try to hang out around the area during the evening to see what they can pick up for EVPs (electronic voice phenomenon) and via their cameras. This is not a good idea, as it leaves you open as a target with some heavy and expensive equipment on display.

- Besides visiting Marie Laveau's tomb, make sure to visit one of the most distinctive tombs here, a tomb shaped like a pyramid built by actor **Nicholas Cage**.

- **All Saints Day,** a Catholic celebration held November 1, is a day where some people visit the tombs to give their respects to their ancestors. This day is also known as the ancient Celtic New Year. If visiting on this day, have respect for the locals who are here to visit family members who are near and dear to them. No matter what day you are visiting, also remember to be respectful for the people who are buried here and laid to rest. I've seen some people who visit and treat the cemetery like it was a tourist site, leaving trash behind and making crude and vulgar jokes. This is a cemetery that is open to the public, and the people buried here all have family who would want them to be treated respectfully and reverently at all times. Consider, as you walk through each path, how you would feel if someone was walking by the gravesites of your loved ones.

- **Save Our Cemeteries** is a nonprofit group in New Orleans who works to preserve these cities of the dead, which are national treasures in both historic and architectural value. If you feel so inspired after visiting the cemetery, consider making a donation to its cause to continue the preservation work. One of the projects it is working on, which I find very exciting, is to restore the tombs to their original Creole colors, rather than the whitewashed versions you see today. Can you imagine how colorful this would look to see the tombs in their traditional shades of lavender, green, and beige in the city of the dead?

- **Bring your camera.** The architecture is so stunning that you'll find yourself wanting to take photos at every turn.

- Make sure to **leave before the cemetery closes,** typically at 3 p.m. Otherwise, you could be locked inside. While the ghosts appear to be polite, legends abound regarding disturbed tombs in the area, which some claim to be frequented by vampires.

- **The greater New Orleans area has more than 40 cemeteries,** most of which are worth a visit. For the sake of this book, I was only able to briefly cover some of the cemeteries in order to write about all the other activities in the city. To truly do them the justice, the cemeteries would require an entire book dedicated to covering them all.

- **Redbrick dust** was gathered from bricks in the cemetery that had crumbled over time. The crumbling bricks were rubbed and the resulting dust was gathered in bags. Voodoo practitioners spread this dust in a straight line in front of a home that needed protection.

- **Visiting cemeteries can deplete your auric energy,** especially if you are an intuitive, medium, or empathic in nature, as you will be sensitive to the grieving energy stored in these locations. When you visit, whether to enjoy the architecture or to see if the spirits are willing to communicate, remember afterward to "shake off" the energy. This is best done by stamping your feet outside the entrance to shake off any of the dirt that may have stuck to your shoes. Next have something sweet to eat to ground your body; chocolate or fruit works best. When you return back to your hotel, take a shower and visualize the water washing away the energy of the day and removing any residual energy that may have attached to you. Then surround your body with pure white light and see your body refreshed and energized. This should restore your energy and prepare you for a night out in NOLA.

Who's Haunting the Garden District?

"In the spring of 1988, I returned to New Orleans, and as soon as I smelled the air, I knew I was home. It was rich, almost sweet, like the scent of jasmine and roses around our old courtyard. I walked the streets, savoring that long-lost perfume."

—Anne Rice, *Interview with the Vampire*

IF YOU ASK A LOCAL IN NEW ORLEANS for directions, be prepared to hear the descriptive terms *uptown* and *downtown,* rather than *east* and *west.* The dividing line is Canal Street, with the French Quarter being downtown. On the other side of Canal Street is the area called uptown, along with the historically beautiful Garden District. Living up to its name, the area is filled with lush fragrant gardens linked with ancient oak trees and the heavenly scents of jasmine, magnolias, day lilies, oleander, honeysuckle, wisteria, crepe myrtles, roses, mimosas, and hundreds of other flora and fauna so luscious that I lost count of them all as I wandered from street to street.

The historic Garden District was established for the American settlers and German, Irish, and other European groups to build beautiful antebellum homes and mansions and to create an area where they would feel welcome. These groups were looked down upon by the French Creoles who lived in the French Quarter and were not welcome to integrate into the Creole society, so the European groups decided to snub the Creoles right back and build elaborate homes and gardens showcasing their wealth and prestige to the French. Next to the Garden District is uptown, where beautiful plantations were built close to the Mississippi River to take advantage of the breezes blowing in from the moving water.

Out of every dark cloud comes a silver lining, as the old saying goes, and this war between the European cultures and classes led to the creation of one of the most beautiful areas in New Orleans, with stunning architectural details both inside and outside the homes. The district was designed by New Orleans architect Barthelemy Lafon, who centered the homes on expansive gardens, giving the area its name. The lush gardens also warded off an occasional problem from the nearby riverfront area, where cattle pens and slaughterhouses in the summer created certain quality of life issues. The gardens worked double duty as they offset these highly unpleasant odors, filling the air with the most pleasant fragrances possible.

Like most homes in New Orleans, many of the Garden District residences report a ghost or two haunting the abodes. In a town this rich in mayhem and zest for life, it's not surprising that some residents remain in spirit to enjoy the home of their dreams after a lifetime of hard work.

The city is magical and stirs the creative juices, as if muses were calling them forth to be reborn. It's no wonder that so many artists, musicians, and authors visit as often as possible and long to call this area home. Hearing the call of my own inner muse suggesting that I make New Orleans my home, I strolled through the streets of the Garden District. Lost in thought, I found myself standing on First Street in front of the former home of Anne Rice, where she wrote *The Witching Hour*. Anne's vivid descriptions of location and surroundings pull the reader into the story, and they are transported here in New Orleans. Strolling past the street is as close as most will come to investigating any of the haunted reports in these homes, though I half

The Garden District lives up to its beautiful name, as depicted in this artist's rendering painted on an antique wood chair.

expected to see the ghost of Deirdre from Anne's book, sitting on the porch in a rocking chair.

During my travels through the Garden District, I met a ghost when I least expected it, riding on the St. Charles streetcar with me. The streetcar is my favorite way to travel through New Orleans, and I have to ride this line every time I'm in the city. The St. Charles streetcar runs for 13 miles along a crescent shape, from Carondelet at Canal Street through the majestic areas of the Garden District to Carrollton Avenue. It's the oldest continually running streetcar line in the world, and the cars are in beautiful condition, with mahogany seats and brass fittings. It's a comfy ride as you lower the windows and feel the breeze blowing in as you rush along the tracks. I've ridden this line many times, and it's a great way to view the homes and take pictures. I especially enjoy looking up at the trees as I roll by to see how many trees I can spot with Mardi Gras beads hanging from their branches.

There's always a mixture of people riding the cars. Locals ride on their way home from work, some heading downtown to be dropped off on Canal Street and others switching streetcar lines from Canal to head over to the French Market. I love hopping from line to line to ride the cars. I've had some of the best conversations while riding the streetcars, chatting about the city and catching up on local stories and gossip.

During the streetcar ride when the ghost appeared to me, I didn't recognize him as a ghost at first. He was an elderly man sitting several seats ahead of me, and I didn't pay him much attention. He wore a hat and was dressed in a suit like some elderly men still do. While I thought it was charming, my attention had been drawn into a wonderful conversation with a delightful African-American woman sitting next to me. She had been sharing stories with me about her life and her ancestors who had lived here, along with stories about her children, who she prayed would be safe while they lived and worked elsewhere. Her deepest prayer was that they would return to New Orleans to live here again. While we didn't delve into the topic of the supernatural in our conversation, I could sense that she had intuitive abilities and saw that many of her ancestors were around her in spirit, watching over her as we chatted.

As we approached her stop, she wished me a good afternoon and then stood up and walked to the exit door. As she did, she briefly stopped next to where the elderly man was seated and paused for a moment as if she was confused. She stood still and looked around, and on this very warm day, she shivered. Clutching her purse tightly to her chest, she looked around once again and then quickly departed the car. I waved to her from the window, but she didn't look back and was walking very quickly away from the car. I turned my attention back inside to see what might have frightened her and why she paused so suddenly. The car was almost empty now, with only a few people still on the car with me. The elderly gentleman was still sitting in the same seat up ahead, and as I looked in his direction, I saw him momentarily disappear and then appear again. I then realized that I had missed this earlier. Because he was a ghost, the lady I had been chatting with couldn't see him, but she felt his energy as she passed by the seat, which gave her a fright. While it sounds astonishing that I wouldn't immediately notice a ghost on the streetcar, it's not as surprising as it sounds in New Orleans. Ghosts are literally everywhere in the city, on the streets, in the bars and restaurants, at the hotels, and attending the parades. You'll be hard-pressed to find a place without some type of haunting in the area. Also, the streetcar had been packed with people throughout the ride, and I had been more interested in the conversation I was having with the woman (along with taking in the sights of the homes, as I swoon over the architecture every time I'm in the city).

Now that there were just a few of us in the streetcar, I turned my attention to him to see what he was up to riding in the streetcar. Not long after my attention was directed his way, he turned around, and discerning that I could see him, he stood up and moved closer to me, sitting in the seat directly in front of me, where he could turn to the side and chat with me, like any other passenger in the car. I was relieved that I was alone in this part of the car at the time, for should I want to speak aloud to him, it wouldn't be the first time that people have looked at me with great concern as they saw me whispering to myself and the thin air around me.

He introduced himself to me as Mr. Charles, stating that he was of no relation to the streetcar being on St. Charles; indeed, he said with a smile, he was no saint. He went on to tell me that he was of Italian descent but that he had gone by the name of Mr. Charles to make it easier for people to pronounce his name, rather than his longer Italian name. He also shared with me that unlike other ghosts, he knew that he was dead and knew where he was buried. On rare occasions, he would visit his grave—not so much to see where his bones lay, but rather, he enjoyed going when it was a holiday and groups of people came out to decorate the tombs and spend time there honoring their families. He enjoyed milling about the crowds and taking part of the activity in the cemetery. He said that he had had a good enough life while alive, though he had experienced his share of sadness, including the loss of his wife, who was the love of his life and had died during childbirth. He had mourned her for the rest of his life, choosing never to marry again. She and the child had died during the birth, but they had already had a daughter, who his family helped raise after his wife's death. He has continued to watch over his descendants who still lived in the city, though he sadly bemoaned that many of them had moved away and were now living in New York.

He then told me the story of being at his cemetery during one of these holiday occasions. As he was standing near where his wife was buried, he saw a little girl who became interested in his wife's tomb. He watched her closely, interested in what she was going to do. The young girl, whom he described as wearing a white dress and having long blond hair and blue eyes, was clutching a bouquet of yellow flowers that her mother had given her to hold. As she began to wander over to his wife's burial place, the young girl's mother called to her and instructed her to come back to where the rest of the family were placing their flowers on a family tomb. The young girl replied to her mother that no, she wanted to put her pretty flowers on this lady's tomb, and as the mother watched, the young girl placed the bouquet of yellow flowers in front of his wife's tomb.

Mr. Charles, in his ghostly form, was so touched by this act, one that he had wished he could do that very day. He said that had he been physically able to weep with joy and gratitude, he most certainly would have. Intrigued, he followed the family around for the rest of the day and accompanied them to their home to see where the young girl lived. He decided to check in on this girl on a frequent basis, becoming a guardian for her throughout her life. He assured me that he never got near enough to her to cause her any concern or fright, but many times he had accompanied her in her daily and nightly activities as she grew up, to protect her in any way that he could. As she grew up into womanhood, he said he visited her less and eventually lost touch with her, though he still visits the cemetery and would love to see her there again one day.

It was one of the most poignant, touching, and yet completely normal conversations that I have ever had with a ghost. He was not confused on any level about his current state; he knew he was dead and had chosen to remain here on the earth plane and not cross over. He was aware that time had passed and observed the passing through watching generations of his family and others grow up and move on. He was at peace and happy with his state of being in this half life as a ghost. I asked him why he stayed here in this twilight life, and he said, "This is what I know. What is there in heaven? Beautiful music, sweet smells, laughter, and lush gardens? Why, I have this every day here in New Orleans. This is my heaven. Why would I not stay right here?" I gently suggested that perhaps if he did move on, he could be reunited with his wife whom he missed so dearly. He replied to me that his wife was an angel and that he knew that when he did move on to the other side, that where he would be living in heaven would be no place near where she was allowed to reside.

He spoke fleetingly at this point and became guarded, even looking around to see if anyone could overhear his conversation to me, as he now spoke to me in a whisper. He shared that

Life, death, spirits, drinks, and jazz all blend together in New Orleans.

while he had been a good man, he had been forced into doing some activities that were, as he described them, unsavory. He alluded to the Mafia element in the city, a powerful underworld during his time. Being Italian, he was asked to do some favors for these men, and while it was possible that he could decline their offer, those who did decline were typically found dead or worse. He didn't want to elaborate on what was worse than death, and I didn't want to interrupt his story. He explained that the favors went up a level each time he was asked, and that he had participated in sorrowful activities that haunted him to this day. He had done his best to keep this information secret from his wife as not to worry her, but he said that like most women, she had a way of knowing when something was wrong and questioned him often about why he looked so worried and tired many times. He would shrug it off as the pressures of doing business and then try to distract her with other news of his day.

It was his belief that because of the sins he had committed during his earthly life, he would be living in a lowly place in heaven, if he made it to heaven at all, while his wife was a proverbial saint and would be living in the holiest of holy places in heaven, and that they would not be together over there. Understanding that he was a Catholic, I said that surely he must have gone to confession and asked for forgiveness. He replied that he did many times, but that he knew that this did not truly release his sins for what he had done.

He explained to me that he thought that the best thing he could do was penance, which he tried to do every day by riding the streetcar and looking after the people in the city. He said, with a smile to me, that while he was still just Mr. Charles, perhaps one day, if he did enough good things, he, too, could be called St. Charles like the streetcar he rode.

At this point the streetcar lurched to a stop, shifting everyone in their seats. Some of the brakes on these cars are not the best and the drivers really have to stomp on them at times. As I steadied myself and then settled back in my seat, Mr. Charles was standing and moving away. I looked up at him to see why our conversation had concluded so abruptly, and he pointed to an elderly lady who had just entered the car. "She's one of my regulars," he said as he went to go sit next to her. The next stop was mine, and as I exited, I smiled and whispered as I went by that I hoped to see him again sometime when I was in the city. He smiled and said, "Here in New Orleans, it's highly likely we will meet again." To this day, he is one of the most aware and astute ghosts that I have ever communicated with in my lifetime.

Should you want to meet the ghost of Mr. Charles, take a ride on the St. Charles streetcar and ask aloud, "Mr. Charles, are you along for the ride?" Don't be surprised if he strikes up a conversation with you right there.

⚜ KALA'S TRAVEL TIPS

- **Commanders Palace Restaurant** in the Garden District has the reputation of being haunted by the former owner of the restaurant. Almost any local will share a story with you about experiencing the ghost while dining at the restaurant. Built in 1880, the Brennan family continues to uphold the highest level of service and cuisine, and you'll enjoy the dining experience so much that you'll want to haunt the place yourself in the afterlife.

- **Even vampires love a good funeral.** Jazz funerals and second lines are so adored in New Orleans that author Anne Rice arranged her own mock funeral, which began at Lafayette Cemetery #1 in the Garden District. Anne dressed in an antique wedding gown and was ceremoniously placed in a casket. The funeral procession began with a brass band and huge crowds following Anne in her casket through the streets to the Garden District Book Shop, where she signed her book *Memnoch the Devil* for thousands of her fans. Lafayette Cemetery #1 was also filmed for a scene in the *Interview with the Vampire* movie and was written about in Anne's book *The Witching Hour.*

- Want to eat and party like a local? Favorite Garden District hangouts include **Tipitinas,** named after the song by Professor Longhair; **Jacques-Imos Café** for delicious Creole dishes; the **Domilise Sandwich Shop and Bar** for a great po'boy sandwich; and **The Camellia Grill** for a quick bite at the counter.

- While in this part of the city, a must-see is **Audubon Park and Zoo.** The 400-acre park named for John James Audubon was originally a plantation owned by Etienne de Boré, who discovered how to create granulated sugar from sugar cane and subsequently made his fortune. His legacy of land is now Audubon Park, Zoo, and Golf Course. Plan to spend the day touring this area along with visiting Loyola and Tulane Universities nearby.

- One-way fares on the **streetcars** for St. Charles, Riverfront, and Canal Street are $1.25. For $5 invest in a one-day pass for the streetcars, and you can ride all the cars all day long. The St. Charles streetcar will take you past the beautiful homes and areas of the Garden District, by Loyola and Tulane Universities, and to the Audubon Zoo and Gardens. Take the Canal Streetcar to visit the French Market at one end of the line, and ride it on the 5-mile route to the other end at Canal Street and City Park Avenue to visit many of the historic cemeteries mentioned in this book. The Riverfront Line is a new addition that will carry you from the French Market to the Aquarium of the Americas and to a variety of places to shop and dine. The streetcars here in New Orleans are so romantic and captivating that Tennessee Williams was inspired to write *A Streetcar Named Desire* here in the city.

- In ancient Greek mythology, there were nine Greek goddesses, called **muses,** who ruled and provided inspirations over the arts and sciences. These muses were Calliope (epic poetry), Clio (history), Erato (love poetry), Euterpe (music), Melpomene (tragedy), Polyhymnia (sacred hymns), Terpsichore (dance), Thalia (comedy), and Urania (astronomy). In the Garden District of New Orleans, the streets (designed by city planner and architect at the time, Barthelemy Lafon) are named after each of these muses. The muse streets cross Prytania Street, representing the hearth of the goddess Hestia. Dryades is named for the wood nymphs, and two of the three graces—Euphrosine (joy) and Thalia (flowering)—are streets. For some reason, the third grace, Aglaia (Beauty), is not named.

CHAPTER 3

Tread Carefully When Walking Down the Haunted Pirates Alley

"New Orleans life is such a night life. The thing that comes up very often is that our day essentially doesn't start until midnight or two in the morning."

—Robert Asprin

LOCATED IN THE FRENCH QUARTER at St. Louis Cathedral in Jackson Square are alleyways that run along the left and right side of the cathedral. On the left side (or as directions are given in New Orleans, the uptown side) is Pirates Alley, which is a one-block cobblestone pedestrian walkway located between St. Louis Cathedral and the Cabildo building. The street is easily marked by one of the landmark New Orleans street signs and is one of the most-photographed street signs in New Orleans.

When walking down the street, you feel as though you might discover a hidden treasure or secret bounty—filled with precious gems and rarely seen antique items—spilling from one of the doors you pass by. During the day, it's very busy with people passing through on their way to shops and cafés, with local artists lining the streets to showcase their wares and with performing musicians of all kinds, from solo artists on guitar or saxophone to three-piece bands.

The setting is very romantic and has become one of the most popular outdoor locations to get married in New Orleans, right here in the alley rather than inside St. Louis Cathedral. As you walk along Pirates Alley—filled with music,

Corner of Pirates Alley

tourists, and artists—it's difficult to imagine that this alley once led to the old Spanish jail where prisoners were marched down the street.

The area is every bit as busy today as it was during the days when General Andrew Jackson hurried through the streets under threat of war with the British. In 1813, Pierre Lafitte, brother of the legendary pirate Jean Lafitte, was arrested for the crimes of smuggling and piracy and was imprisoned in the Cabildo building, which is located across from this alleyway. Both brothers were equally culpable of the crimes, but most likely there was more direct evidence against Pierre since Jean handled the actual pirating from the ship and Pierre was in charge of dispersing these goods in the port of New Orleans.

This may sound like a very straightforward case. A crime was committed and the guilty party was placed in jail, but this is not a case of black-and-white/right-and-wrong reasoning.

Pirating was always an interesting profession, and what many people don't realize is that it was a very gray area legally, depending on the political climate of the time.

When war began between the American colonies and Britain in 1812, the American government offered legal papers to many pirates—Lafitte's crew included—giving them the rights and direction to "raid" British ships, the technical term for pirating. The British government also extended this raiding offer to the pirates. This wasn't the only time governments used pirates and gave them the freedom to do their business. On the Atlantic Coast of the United States, Blackbeard the Pirate and others were also many times given free reign to do likewise by various governments at war.

With this in mind, it's easy to imagine that a man who built his business and lifestyle as a pirate would see the gray areas between countries and laws, as both countries would often offer him clemency, removal of criminal records, and legal documents granting him the legal right to do the work he did for years at a time. Once wars were over, the governments would then officially pull these rights and again publicly condemn them as criminals. Yet behind closed doors, clandestine meetings would still occur, where government officials would turn a blind eye to the pirate's activities and provide favors in return for intelligence information against their enemies.

In the case of the arrest of Pierre Lafitte, he and his brother Jean were operating under the permission of the US government to pirate at this time. Somehow this information never seemed to pass far along the chain of command, as the U.S. Navy preferred not to recognize this status of the pirates, creating a double-edged challenge for the pirates, as the enemy of their enemy was never their friend. Complaints by some Navy officials led to laws stating that all contraband obtained by the pirates must be immediately handed over to the US government. Naval officials accused the pirates of keeping treasures and ordered the accused pirates to be arrested on sight. So on a double-cross by the government, both Lafitte brothers were arrested in November 1812. They immediately placed bail and were released until their trial. Not surprisingly, neither brother returned for the trial. In 1813, Pierre, working the risky position of fencing the stolen goods to customers in New Orleans, was an easier target and was captured and placed in jail.

During this time, British intelligence approached Jean Lafitte and asked him to come work for their side. With Jean's brother back in jail, it would have been easy for Lafitte to take his revenge on the US government and help the British, with the agreement that when the British took over the port of New Orleans, his brother would be freed. To his credit, Jean Lafitte declined the British offer, reportedly based on the business decision that his pirating business ran better under the American government, which was still small in comparison and had fewer available resources to hinder his business.

Legend has it that the daring Jean Lafitte risked his own freedom by meeting with the governor of Louisiana in this very alleyway on a dark and stormy night to negotiate his brother's freedom in return for the Lafitte brothers offering information and assistance against the British in the upcoming Battle of New Orleans. He explained to the governor that he had received a substantial offer from the British and offered his allegiance to Louisiana instead. The governor reportedly agreed that it would be best for the Lafittes to be friends of Louisiana rather than to work for the British, and it was arranged that Pierre would be allowed to "escape" from jail in the Cabildo so that no official could be publicly blamed.

The legend continues that Jean Lafitte later met another top-ranking official, General Andrew Jackson, in this alleyway for a similar clandestine meeting. Under the cover of darkness and on a foggy night, it is reported that Jackson offered full legal pardons to both brothers in exchange for their services against the British. The Lafitte brothers agreed and worked as spies, offering intelligence and operating as pirates for the US government. While an alleyway might seem like a strange place to meet, imagine being a wanted man and meeting government officials who are prone to going back on their promises in direct sight of the prison. It's hard to imagine any criminal choosing this area as a preferred meeting site. Yet the legend prevails. The reasons are plentiful, including the sanctuary of the cathedral being only steps away, as well as the cover of darkness and many paths and alleys around the area to aid in an easy escape. Rumors also prevail that at the nearby apartments, there were many women captivated by the romantic and dashing Jean, and the women would provide lookout information and safe places to stow away in troubled times. Pirates were beloved by many people in ports, contrary to what the history books often claim. For many people, their personal businesses profited from the wares smuggled in by these men. During times of war, goods that were impossible to obtain legally were often hand-delivered by the pirates to paying clients. One only has to think of Rhett Butler in *Gone with the Wind* to see how dashing and romantic these men could appear as they delivered goods to those in need.

In the clear light of day, I strolled along Pirates Alley coming from the direction of Bourbon Street. At the end of the alley you arrive on Decatur Street, which leads you to a wonderful treat at Café du Monde. Here you can have a seat and sample world-famous beignets, which are best described as French-style doughnuts served warm and covered in powdered sugar, served up hot on a white plate with a cup of café au lait. Café du Monde provides a stunning view of Jackson Square, and the breezes coming off the Mississippi River make this one of the most enchanting areas in the city.

Café du Monde is one of my top 10 places to see and be
seen, as the people-watching is incredible. Everything changes
constantly here, as people move in and out of the café amid performing musicians and street artists. Across the street, horse-
drawn carriages are lined up to take visitors on a tour of the
French Quarter, and artists display canvases against the wrought
iron fence surrounding Jackson Square. St. Louis Cathedral provides an easily recognizable landmark in the square, and it is
surrounded by a lush garden.

Sitting here at Café du Monde creates a distinct moment
in time. As I relax and savor the beignets, the coffee, and the
music, I realize that I have become part of the scene and part of
the history here, as does each person with his or her presence at
this moment. The mood is complex and intriguing; it is every
bit relaxing while also strangely energizing due to the music and
the movement of people. One has a sense of being somewhere
special and in the midst of life as it should be. People from every
walk of life you can imagine are mixing together: bohemians,
artists, professionals, travelers, children, seniors, along with a
few writers thrown into the mix.

The scene is one of chaos blended into bliss, where each
note of jazz played by rotating artists at the café carries the
people along from day into evening. To my delight, I find that
the energy of the music and the people moving in and out
of the café are an exotic representation of this same movement,
which is delightful. I am experiencing a moment of heaven on
earth, where the spiritual planes open and the veil is so thin
that those here on earth can easily bump into angels and spirits from the other side.

I've been to Café du Monde more times than I can count
over my many visits to New Orleans. This time I'm here to experience something new—I'm waiting for twilight, the "tween"
time. Mystical practitioners know that the one-hour time period

Café du Monde, where the author spent time eating beignets while waiting for sunset. Pontalba Apartments in the background.

during sunrise and sunset is the easiest time to slip through the veils and commune with spirits on the other side and those who remain here on the earth plane.

I'm choosing this time to connect with the spirit world because during the day as I travel through Pirates Alley, it is so crowded and busy with people that it would be hard to discern who is a ghost and who is a local. So I wait, sipping my coffee and letting the spirit of New Orleans wash over me note by note.

Sunset soon falls, and the crowds begin to disperse. The café thins out, and the waiters take this opportunity to sweep up some of the mounds of powdered sugar that waft across tables and the floor. Jackson Square seems to sigh deeply with a long breath as vendors pack up their art to head home, and musicians pick up their instruments and move over to Bourbon Street to play on the streets to the nightly crowds. The café doesn't close;

it remains open 24 hours a day, seven days a week, as a beacon of light and warmth in the quarter. Come here at midnight or at 3 a.m. and the seats will be filled with those who are wrapping up their night from the bars and the bands, locals who are enjoying coffee after a late dinner, and others who prefer the night as their companion.

As the energy of the city shifts during sunset, it's a prime time to walk again along the alley. This time as I walk along Pirates Alley, I am no longer fighting hordes of people with small children, strollers, and shopping bags. I am not bombarded by the sounds that humans make with hundreds of voices mixed in with musical notes played by the street musicians. Now, here in the quiet, it's the night and me. In the dark with the streetlamps offering their gentle light, I open myself psychically and ask that should there be anyone here in spirit who wishes to communicate, they are welcome to do so now.

Admittedly, I do this with some trepidation. Jackson Square, though beautiful as it is today, was historically the site of public executions for many years in New Orleans. Execution sites are well known for restless spirits, and I'm not sure what type or how many spirits I may meet here in the still of the night when I put out the call.

Extending my hands outward, I raise my protective white light shield around me, which accomplishes two goals; it creates a layer of protection around my aura to ward off any forces that I don't want to come too near and brightens my auric light, which will be noticed easily by those in the otherworldly planes. This is a good technique to use to attract attention and can be seen for miles by those in the supernatural world. This can attract beings from both sides who may have an interest in checking out a bright energy source, like moths to a flame.

Opening myself up to the experience, I wait to see who responds to my call. At first, all is quiet and still, which surprises me. I grow impatient and, after a minute or two, let down my guard, which is a mistake. Seconds later, a wave of energy washes over me, and I'm now seeing Pirates Alley as it was in the past. Something here wants me to see their life but isn't willing to show themselves to me directly. I look around, hoping to see the figure that is engaging with me, but have no luck. The alley appears much darker and quieter at night now than it did in my time, though I can hear the shouting of two men in the far distance.

As I walk farther down the alley, I make out a shadowy figure in the distance. As I get closer, I see a woman sobbing, nearly bent over in grief, holding her arms around her waist as if to support her body from falling to the ground. Her head hangs low and tendrils of her hair have loosened and are falling on each side of her face. She's cold and appears weary to her core. As I draw closer, she looks up at me with tears streaming down her face. She shouts at me angrily in loud bursts of French. Growing up in Louisiana, I picked up some of the French language, but it was a less proper form of Cajun French, which sounds quite different from the formal French flowing out of her at a rapid pace.

As a psychic, people often ask me how can I understand what ghosts and spirits are saying when they speak in a foreign language, as I only speak English. The best way I can describe this is that in the other planes of existence of the spirit world, language is a pattern of light and sound with its own formula of creation that is quite beautiful; the language is expressed telepathically rather than verbally.

As the young woman on Pirates Alley continued to scream at me in French, I took a deep breath and calmed myself down. I was intrigued by her language and had allowed myself to become both fascinated and captivated. I needed to take a step back and experience what she was expressing to me. As I did,

I saw the image of the young man who was her lover. She was not married to this man, nor did her family approve of their relationship. She was from a family of higher standing and he was not French. Undeterred, the young lovers had continued to meet and had been securing funds to elope. The young woman had reached out to an uncle and aunt whom she had thought were sympathetic to her cause, as her uncle had married a woman who was not of the same social class. Trusting them, she had shared her plans about eloping. To her great surprise, her uncle was against the idea. He told her that while he had married his love, he also had the means to raise his wife up in social standing; as a woman, she would never be able to raise the social standing of her young lover and would surely be disowned and disinherited by her family should she proceed further with her plans.

The young woman left her uncle's home angry, but with the belief that he would keep her secret safe. This proved to be an error in judgment on her part. After she left, her uncle's wife went to her parents and betrayed her secret to them, hoping to raise her own standing within the family by delivering this news. The young woman's father then devised a plan to stop this engagement at once and used his considerable resources to have the young man arrested on what were false pretenses.

She pleaded with her father day and night to have the young man released. She swore that if he did, she would never see him again, wishing only for his freedom. She would give up her desire to marry him if only her father would grant her this one wish. She offered to go to a convent or marry any man of her father's choosing. However, her father refused to relent, and the young man stayed in jail. About a month later, she learned through sources that her lover had died in jail. It was unclear what had occurred. Some said it was natural causes; others said he had contracted a terrible fever and died of some disease, and others claimed he had tried to escape and was killed by guards.

She did not know which story was true, but she suspected that her father had something to do with her lover's death since she had not given up her daily vigil of pleading with him to release him from jail. Through death, her father had complied with her wish of setting her lover free, but not in the way she had intended. She never knew what truly happened, as there was no burial announcement that she could find and no one could tell her what happened to his body. She continued to come to this area night after night, hoping that he had escaped and would find her at St. Louis Cathedral. This never came to pass, and she decided the only way to find him again would be to join him in the afterlife.

As she looked up at me with tears streaming down her face, I noticed that her eyes were glazed over and that her arms were wrapped tightly around her waist. She was experiencing severe abdominal pain from having taken some form of poison, which was working its way through her body. Her sobbing was from both physical and emotional pain, as she was experiencing what she remembered at the end of her life. Even now in her ghostly form, she still clung to this pain in the afterlife. I spoke softly to her and asked why she was here in the alley instead of in front of St. Louis Cathedral, where she had arranged to meet her young man. She told me that she could not stand near the front door of the cathedral because taking her own life was a sin.

As gently as I could, I explained to her that she did not have to remain here in pain and grief. She could move on to the other side and find her lover waiting for her there. She told me that only bad things waited for her on the other side because of what she had done, and she remained here hoping he would find her. I told her that she had been waiting long enough and that if she could move on, she would find him there on the other side. She replied that she had only been waiting for a short while, and she was sure he would find her soon.

This is often the case with ghosts; they are truly unaware of how much time has passed since their death. She had no idea of how many years had gone by while she remained in this half-life world of grief and despair. When I explained to her that she had been waiting for a very long time, she swore at me and said she did not believe me. I asked her then to look at me, to really look closely at me, and look at my clothing to see that I was speaking to her from another time. She slowly placed her gaze on me and swore in shock, seeing that I was a woman wearing pants. Gaining her trust and piqued interest, I invited her to look around at the shops, the lights, and the street to see how things had changed over time. The realization began to wash over her, and she broke free from her spell of grief in frozen time. What happened next is something that makes me weep with joy every time I think of it and as I write it here today.

As she stared in amazement of what I was showing her, a figure in the distance approached us slowly. The movement caught my eye, and as I turned my gaze to see who was approaching us, the young woman noticed I had stopped communicating with her and also turned to see what I was looking at in the alley.

The figure grew closer, and with a gasp, the young woman softly asked, "Me're?" The figure, now standing in front of us, smiled and held out her arms to her daughter. The young woman, still reeling from anger, shock, and grief, paused for a moment and then fell into her mother's loving arms. Embracing her daughter, the mother looked over at me and sent me an energetic impulse, which I can only describe as a wave of gratitude. The young woman was crying again, this time in the safety of her mother's arms, and the mother began to cry in relief, as only a mother can understand her eternal love for her child. At this point, I began to cry. As an empath, I felt the emotional intensity of this experience, as well as an understanding as a mother and a daughter myself.

Pulling her child away gently from her arms, she spoke lovingly to her daughter and said, "It's time to go home." The daughter looked at her in fear and asked if she truly could go home with her mother. Her mother—a beautiful, strong, and regal woman—wiped away her child's tears, tucked the tendrils of loose hair behind her daughter's ears, and told her indeed, she was sure that she could come home. Taking her daughter's hand, the two set off down the alley and soon disappeared from my sight into a beautiful field of white light.

A mother's love is eternal and knows no bounds; not even death and traveling through the spiritual planes can stop her for coming to rescue her child. My feeling about the situation was that the mother had tried many times before to reach out to her child over the years, but in the state of overwhelming grief that the young girl had stayed in, she was hidden in a dark gray plane of existence that made her difficult to locate by others in spirit. When they did locate her, it would be hard to communicate with her in such a state of grief and pain.

I had no clue where the young girl had actually died, or if her body had ever been found. She indicated that she had not passed on here in the alley and explained to me that she traveled here each night in the hopes of finding her lover. My best assumption in experiencing other cases like this is that if the young girl had been buried in the family vault, her mother would have been able to reach her there at some time. So it's likely that the girl went out into the wilderness after taking the poison and died alone. This cannot be confirmed, though, as it is also possible that the young girl had been found and was buried elsewhere off of consecrated ground, as church doctrines did not allow for suicides to be buried on holy grounds. During my time with the young girl, I did not think that a discussion of this sort would best serve her in the brief time that I had to spend with her. Even if the mother had visited the grave that was located elsewhere, it is likely that the young girl would have hidden from her in the shame of the circumstances regarding her death.

In her moment of clarity when we spoke and she realized that time had indeed passed by for longer than she had imagined, her energy lifted from the grief, making her spirit easier to locate by her mother, whom I believed had long been searching for her daughter each night.

It's unknown at this time if the young woman has been reunited with her long-lost love in the afterlife. I hope to bump into them one day when I'm on the other side, and if I do, I plan to treat them to a café au lait and some beignets together, as the Café du Monde is so delightful that there surely must be one open 24 hours a day in the heavens.

Kala's Travel Tips

- I was weary after this experience and needed to ground back down to the earth plane again and replenish my energy, so there were no more ghostly explorations on this night. **Pirates Alley,** though, is very supernaturally active. I highly recommend that paranormal researchers visit it, especially for EVP recordings, due to the many executions that occurred nearby. I plan to check it out again on my next visit.

- If I haven't made this clear already, a visit to **Café du Monde** is a must-do for too many reasons to mention. Visit at sunrise for breakfast to see the city as it shines in the morning, visit again in the evening to see how it relaxes at night, and visit again at noon to take in all the lively action!

- The shops around Pirates Alley still hold valuable treasures, including the works of great literary figures such as Nobel Laureate William Faulkner. The **Faulkner House** is located on 624 Pirates Alley and is a national landmark. Faulkner lived here in true New Orleans style, enjoying the music, the food, and the cocktails, and reportedly fell in love on the balcony here on the home. He also wrote here, and his books can be found on the ground floor at **Faulkner House Books.**

- **Weather** can play havoc in the area when looking to use photography for paranormal investigations. I've been at Pirates Alley when it's a beautiful clear sunny day only to see it enveloped in fog only a few hours later that night.

CHAPTER 4

Ghostly Harem Dancing for the Sultan at the Gardette– LePrete House

"Tis now the very witching time of night,/ when churchyards yawn and hell itself breathes out/contagion to this world."

—William Shakespeare, *Hamlet*

ONE OF THE MOST INTERESTING and defining aspects of New Orleans is how cosmopolitan the city has always been. Since its inception, the city has attracted settlers, business-people, and travelers from all parts of Europe, the Caribbean islands, and the Far East. This leads us to the legendary tale of one dark and stormy night around the year 1878, when a mysterious ship arrived in the port of New Orleans under the cover of darkness.

When the storm passed that evening, those who ventured out onto the streets were treated to a strange and highly unusual sight, which is saying something profound given what all can be viewed on a daily basis in New Orleans. On this night, a Middle Eastern sultan, whom some said was a prince, disembarked from his vessel, which was laden with trunks, furniture, tapestries, carpets, and an entourage of guards who carried swords and pistols. Completely surrounded by guards as they walked down the street was the sultan's harem, described as bejeweled and veiled women wearing luxurious silk clothing in vibrant colors.

The sultan prince had made arrangements to live at one of the grandest homes in New Orleans, which was known as the

Gardette–LePrete House. Located at 716 Dauphine Street on the corner of Orleans Avenue, the four-story home was considered palatial by the standards of this time in New Orleans, featuring extensive and ornate ironwork on the balcony railings and a ballroom with a view on the top floor.

Originally built by Dr. Joseph Coulon Gardette, it was later sold to Jean Baptiste Le Prete, who owned the home along with a large plantation outside of the city in Plaquemines Parish. Reportedly Le Prete used the home in New Orleans only when the family came in for what was described as the social season, when they hosted elaborate parties and attended Creole functions in the French Quarter. When Le Prete learned through an associate that a sultan was interested in renting his home during the off-season, he reportedly jumped at the chance to rent out the home, as his personal finances were not the best at this time, and he welcomed the extra income. Little did he realize what would happen next and that he would soon shudder and be forever repulsed at the thought of ever returning to his home again.

Upon their arrival in New Orleans, the sultan and his people busied themselves settling into the home, rolling out their exotic and beautiful carpets, unpacking furniture, and shopping for luxurious goods from the local stores. The women could be seen passing by the expansive windows of the home and at times standing along the iron balconies to enjoy the sunlight and fresh air. The interested residents of New Orleans often strolled by the home, hoping to catch a glimpse of the harem women. Many members of the French Creole society entertained ideas of soon receiving invitations by the sultan prince to attend a ball or other formal function at his home as he introduced himself to New Orleans society.

It soon became apparent that social invitations would not be forthcoming. To the surprise of many, the windows were shuttered and the guards, who had completed their tasks of

Entrance to the Gardette–LePrete House

unloading trunks and furniture, now turned their attention to securing all points of entry to the home, stationing themselves outside the main door and gate to patrol the area day and night. The guards were described as menacing in their appearance, and they carried swords and knives at all times. Gossip began to circulate that the sultan had escaped from the country he called home with great treasures and a harem that belonged to another prince. The rumors spread that it was his brother who was the sultan prince and that he had betrayed his brother, stolen his wealth and his harem, and escaped the country. He was on the run, they said, and felt that the New World, specifically New Orleans, would be the best place to hide out and lay low for a while until he determined his next move.

Locals were now even more intrigued by the rumors and gossip regarding the sultan. They walked by the property day and night, longing to get a peek into the windows when the guards weren't looking to see what was transpiring inside. Fanciful stories about the beautiful harem women grew each night, as sounds of music and laughter carried through the starlight nights into the streets. Locals reported seeing the women wearing small coins in belts on their hips that tinkled as they danced for the sultan. Each story grew more lavish, including stories about silks lining the walls in every room, and the women became more beautiful and charming with each new description. Many continued to hope that when the sultan felt safe and comfortable in his new surroundings, he would venture into the city with his harem and invite guests into his home to experience the exotic food, drink, and dancing.

This elaborate party, however, did not come to pass. One night, under a dark moon said to be very similar to the evening when the sultan's ship first arrived in port, a deep fog rolled into New Orleans, and a strange ship that could not be easily identified was seen offshore. The ship appeared to drop anchor in the sea, and it was assumed that it would not venture closer until the fog lifted and visibility was clear, so that it could carefully enter the port without the threat of damage to the ship or the docks.

Under these stormy skies in the French Quarter during the wee hours of the morning, a group of men left a local bar and took their nightly stroll by the sultan's palace. They were hoping that under the cover of the dense fog, they might slip past the guards and peer through one of the windows to glimpse the women dancing in their exotic veils. To their surprise, as the sunrise began to spread the first rays of light over the city, the highly patrolled front gate was unguarded, and the men were greeted by the cold chill of silence. It was eerily quiet without the usual sounds of music and laughter pouring from the windows, and no guards were in sight. Some of the men crept closer to peek through the gates, and as they drew near, they saw pools of blood on the ground. Alarmed, they called the authorities to the scene. The police attempted to rouse the guards. When no one appeared, they entered the property.

According to the legendary story, what they found next was bloodshed and gruesome mayhem in every corner. The sultan's guards had all been brutally sexually molested and then murdered. It appeared that their own swords had been used to not only kill them, but also to chop off their body parts bit by bit, as their arms, legs, and heads had all been severed in the bloodbath. Moving deeper through the home and into the courtyard area, the police found the sultan, who had been brutally tortured and wounded in such a vile manner that most of the officers on duty would not fully describe the depth of the injuries and wounds, but indicated that he had been tortured beyond the extreme with no mercy. They reported that he had been kept from death at first, in order to be buried alive in the most torturous manner, so that his last moments of life were sheer agony between the pain of his wounds and suffocating to death. The police were soon to find the worst scene of all when they discovered the women, who had been raped and brutally murdered next to their children. Blood splatters covered the courtyard and the balconies, and pools of blood covered the floors throughout the home. The destruction was so severe that it was said that the coroner could not accurately determine which body parts belonged to each body when it came time for the burials.

It was a scene of complete devastation. Along with the brutal murders, all personal belongings and furniture in the home had also been destroyed and hacked to bits, and any evidence of gold and jewels had disappeared. At first, police speculated that the motive was robbery, but this was quickly dismissed as the attacks themselves were entirely too personal. Too much time had been spent on torturing the victims rather than attempting to steal the possessions and make a quick getaway.

Balcony and courtyard area of the Gardette–LePrete House

The next morning, the strange ship that had been seen off the coast the night before had vanished with the fog. It was determined that the prince whom the sultan had attempted to escape from had found him in New Orleans. Consumed with revenge, the prince had sent a team of the cruelest, most bloodthirsty assassins, who crept into the port under the cover of darkness and unleashed their fury on the sultan and all those who lived with him.

Under the next new moon, the hauntings began to be reported at the LePrete home. At first, the sound of music was heard playing, along with the laughter of women. These sounds quickly changed into screams, and some people reported being able to see the women running away in terror from the balconies before they were knocked to the ground.

The home has reportedly never recovered from the dark events that it witnessed. Many people say that if you walk by the home on a dark moon night, you will hear these shrieks of terror. I walked by the house and found the building to be quiet while I was on the street. I spoke with several local people in the area who told me that they and others have heard the sound of music coming from the building before, and they described the music as not coming from a radio and not sounding like jazz or blues, like one would expect to hear playing in the area. They describe the music as having a ting, ting, ting sound. There are also reports of some local witnesses seeing women in beautifully colored silks appearing on the balcony late at night.

It would be fascinating to gain permission to tour the building for a couple of hours on a new moon evening. As active as this place is described and with as much bloodshed that reportedly occurred there, it's very likely that researchers could pick up some interesting EVP recordings. It's doubtful at this time that permission would be granted, as the home is a private residence that has been turned into apartments for rent. Haunted tours do offer walking tours and carriage rides outside the home, where the guides share the legend and story of the sultan prince. Some of the guides report that people continue to hear spectral sounds, including music, footsteps dancing, laughter, and, at other times, screams, coming from inside the building at night.

⚜ KALA'S TRAVEL TIPS

- The LePrete house is architecturally interesting to see with its beautiful ironwork balconies. **Consider taking photos by day and at night** in order to capture the look of the building as a souvenir. While doing so, you may end up with a ghostly photo or two.

- Also located on Dauphine Street is the **Dauphine Orleans Hotel,** which is home to the famous Audubon Cottage, where John James Audubon painted his *Birds of America* series in 1822. While you're there, check out **May Baily's,** the bar in the hotel named after one of the most famous bordellos in New Orleans, which once operated in the historic red-light Storyville District.

- The **port of New Orleans** is still one of the nation's busiest ports, as ships roll in from the Mississippi River as well as from the Gulf of Mexico daily. Many visitors to the city enjoy spending a few days in New Orleans and then boarding one of the cruise lines to see the Caribbean, traveling in a grander style than the pirates and early settlers did on the high seas.

CHAPTER 5

Marie Laveau—The Legendary Queen of Voodoo

"Stir the fire till it lowe
How like a Queen comes forth the lonely Moon
From the slow-opening curtains of the clouds,
Walking in beauty to her midnight throne!"

—George Croly, "Diana"

VOODOO ARRIVED IN NEW ORLEANS during the antebellum period, as the people of Africa brought their spiritual practices and customs to the New World. As new arrivals entered the city from Africa, Haiti, and the Caribbean islands, these cultures blended and shared their magical secrets, enhancing them with new ingredients, spells, and practices to strengthen the rituals and incantations.

Out of this combination of cultures, a new form of Voodoo arose, which differs from the strictly Haitian Voodoo and from the various West African practices. Many refer to this style as Louisiana Voodoo, which focuses on the women as the high priestess and queen of the group who holds court and is recognized as the supreme leader. Items that are unique to the Louisiana style of Voodoo include Voodoo dolls and gris-gris bags, which are bags filled with charms such as botanicals and other organic ingredients carefully selected and blended to bring power, magic, and mojo to the bearer of these bags. Gris-gris bags were made for specific purposes, including attracting love and providing holistic healing. The bags would often include therapeutic oils and medicinal herbs, and the patient would be instructed to wear the bag on their body to allow the oils to seep through the skin into the body for healing. This type of traditional folk medicine was also used in ancient Celtic traditions and other wise woman folk healings throughout Europe. Gris-gris bags were made for money and prosperity, health and wellness, love and relationships, and specially ordered magical bags were prepared for protection, dreams, and luck, as well as to develop psychic powers and to clear and remove negative energy from homes and businesses.

As these practices grew in New Orleans, the structure of Louisiana Voodoo shifted and changed as it melded into the unique mixture of French, Spanish, African, and Caribbean cultures in the city. Catholicism was the predominant religion in the area. With many similarities between the two religions, including the appreciation of the divine feminine and praying to a variety of spiritual beings for help, over time the Catholic practices were adopted into Voodoo rituals. It was an easy cross-connection for practitioners to align the concept of their helpful spirit gods with the representation of the saints of the Catholic church.

People from all walks of life, religions, and cultures were known to use Voodoo as needed in New Orleans. The concept was not considered foreign, as praying to the Voodoo gods for protection, love, and personal needs was considered to be very similar to the Catholic doctrines of praying to the saints in times of need. Both practices lit candles, said prayers, carried rosaries or prayer beads, used incense and oils in various practices for blessings, and wore lucky and blessed charms, such as the St. Christopher medal for protection.

In Congo Square on Sundays, the slaves in New Orleans gathered to dance, socialize, play music, and pass along secrets and confidential information while selling their wares for profit. A great variety of handmade arts and crafts items were always available, including Voodoo products and supplies that were

**Voodoo dolls
purchased
by the author**

always in high demand. A unique variety of ingredients were required to create protection spells and gris-gris bags. Many items were labor intensive, such as gathering redbrick dust from cemeteries and obtaining certain items from the swamps under various phases of the moon. At times, bones, feathers, and other bits of animals were required for specific rituals, and those who were willing to gather these items could turn a profit in selling them.

Voodoo ran through the city using a powerful communication network mostly run by the women. Free women of color operated shops for dressmaking, to sell jewelry and adornments, and to provide hairstyling services. These positions allowed them front-row access to the Creole women from the highest echelons of society. Spending time in the company of these wealthy women as they styled their hair and made clothes for them, they would hear the local gossip, along with the problems faced by these women and their families. A great majority of the time, the shop owners and hairdressers would be asked to travel to their client's home to style her hair before a big event and deliver dresses, hats, and gloves. This provided the shopkeepers and stylists the opportunity to not only hear the society gossip but also to chat with the servants in the home, who provided even greater detailed information to these women. This gave these free women of color a tremendous advantage of knowing who was ill, who was having marital infidelities, who was unable to conceive, and who was experiencing financial troubles. The women were able to take this information and suggest various Voodoo remedies and cures to their clients to help with the situation at hand.

The Woman, the Legend, the Queen

Ask anyone who has ever paid the slightest attention to the world of Voodoo what they know about the subject and chances are that the name Marie Laveau will be the main topic of discussion. Regarded as the queen high priestess of Voodoo in New Orleans, Marie was respected by all who knew her. Her reputation was so revered that even her enemies thought twice before taking her on in any manner. Marie was a free person of color and regarded as one of the best hairstylists in town. The majority of her clients were the wealthy French women in the city, who were said to adore her. She quickly gained their trust and confidence by making poultices and spells that helped with the pain of childbirth, as well as making women more fertile so that they could conceive more children. On the flip side, when some women came to her no longer desiring to have children, she

Marie Laveau has the most visited tomb in all of New Orleans.

provided contraception methods that helped them achieve these goals as well. Her reputation grew quickly throughout the city, and women sought her services for love, health, children, and protection. This allowed Marie, along with other female Voodoo practitioners, to build up a strong and extremely valuable network through the city, bringing clients to her on a daily basis and allowing her to make a comfortable living as an entrepreneur.

While Marie and other practitioners like her provided the mundane practices of Voodoo to clients, delivering potions and gris-gris bags as needed, the more elaborate rituals were held in the swamps outside the city as well as at Bayou St. John, where spiritual ceremonies were conducted (including the high priestesses dancing naked to a powerful rhythm of drums while handling large serpents).

The most famous Voodoo festival held each year is during summer solstice, which is also referred to as St. John's Festival. Many times, these festivals are open to the public to attend and observe. During the time that Marie Laveau reigned as the queen of Voodoo, she often invited reporters and the public to attend and witness the festivities on Bayou St. John and on Lake Pontchartrain. It was said in the early 1870s that more than 12,000 people attended these rituals each year.

Male Voodoo priests exist in other forms of Voodoo, and many ritualistic parts of the Voodoo practice are used with the combination of the feminine and masculine energies. In New Orleans for the most part, it was the women who possessed the power, which gave rise to the term Voodoo queens. Most high priestesses were able to connect with the divine masculine energy of the gods through their rituals and draw this energy down into the ceremony, as was done with the rituals of the high priestesses of ancient Egypt.

Over time the Voodoo hierarchy settled into an organized system in New Orleans, with the Voodoo queens as the high-ranking priestesses followed by the Voodoo doctors, though queens often operated in both roles. The distinction was that the queen ran the important ceremonies and rituals, including the dances. Doctors prepared gris-gris bags along with potions, powders, spells, and other charms and amulets for a variety of ailments and purposes. While the intention of many practitioners, including Marie Laveau, was to create traditional folk remedies and cures using white magic to assist with healing and bring peace and prosperity to clients, other practitioners worked with dark magic and offered talismans and other remedies to cause grave misfortune, discomfort, and ruin to one's enemies as long as the price was paid. These types of ritual magic required physical offerings, including human hair, nail clippings, and other biological material—which at times included blood and parts of animals, with a particular emphasis on snakes, lizards, and frogs. Other more sophisticated rituals include animal organ parts, such as a beef heart for love spells. These black magic gris-gris bags crafted by the practitioner would be given to the person seeking revenge, who would then place this gris-gris bag near the front door of his or her enemy or, if possible, under the enemy's bed. Should the enemy discover the bag and understand the laws of Voodoo, the person would know not to touch the bag. Instead he or she would seek out another Voodoo practitioner to provide a talisman or bag to negate and counteract the black magic, neutralizing the energy and, in some cases, sending the energy back to the source from which it came. Some practitioners walked a fine line in the gray magic area, providing white magic on most occasions while also dipping into dark magic for protective spells when a person was being threatened.

As the legendary Voodoo queen of Louisiana, Marie Laveau was known for her physical beauty, for her skill as a hairdresser, and as a priestess who walked the gray line of magic where she overwhelmingly produced results for her clients. These talents put her in the good graces and confidences of almost everyone in New Orleans, as well as earning the respect of her peers. Her legendary skills grew as a Voodoo queen, and, as her reputation spread, she was called in to service all over the city.

One day she was asked to visit the office of a very wealthy and established man in New Orleans who asked for her assistance. His son had been arrested for a crime which the father knew he was innocent of, but the police claimed they had enough evidence to prove his guilt. The man felt that his son had been set up for a variety of political and economic reasons, and he had no other discourse available than to result to Voodoo to help his son out of the situation. Marie agreed to assist the man with the matter and spent three days in preparation, becoming deeply involved in an intense series of rituals, incantations, spells, and charms. On the third day of the ritual, just hours before the trial was set to be held, Marie placed three hot peppers in her mouth and walked through the French Quarter to the St. Louis Cathedral. When she arrived in the church, she knelt and prayed in the church for an hour, while keeping the hot peppers burning inside her mouth, asking for divine intervention for the plight of this man's son.

She left the church, and through her elaborate system of connections throughout the city, she was able to gain entrance undetected inside the courtroom where the judge would sit to preside over the case. Marie was able to place the hot peppers along with other magical items she had prepared directly under his chair. She then exited the courtroom and reportedly returned home to continue her prayers to the gods to correct the situation now occurring at the courthouse.

The trial began, and despite the overwhelming amount of evidence produced by the police toward the young man, the judge ruled in the young man's favor and pronounced him not guilty. The legend around this event says that the father was so elated by Marie's magic that he not only paid her more than the price she had asked, but he also bought her a small cottage home in appreciation. Other historians dispute this part of the legend, stating that Marie already owned the cottage, which had been handed down from her grandmother. Records during this time were spotty at best, and it has never been fully confirmed exactly when Marie became the owner of this cottage on St. Ann Street. Some historians speculate that the man may have paid off what was still owed on the cottage or contributed financially to Marie in other manners.

Regardless of how she was paid for her work, word of Marie's tremendous abilities to sway the minds of the judicial system quickly began to spread through New Orleans from one wealthy family to another. The opportunities for power

and persuasion were very attractive, and other families began
to share their experiences of the magical abilities that Marie
Laveau had produced for them. From this moment, her reputation soared to an even greater height as she became feared as
well as respected and thus was treated well by all people she
encountered throughout the city. It was also reported that
she possessed psychic abilities and could offer counsel at
the levels once reported by the oracles of Greece. It was said
that Marie was able to communicate with the spirit world and
could both deliver and receive messages from the dead.

Special favors were offered to Marie by the wealthy families
to keep her in their good graces should they ever need a political or legal favor of their own. Through the sale of her potions
and gris-gris bags as well as her other work, Marie created a
legacy and a comfortable living that was later passed down to
her daughter, who also went by the name Marie Laveau.

Queen Marie was also highly respected for her charitable
works, and she joined forces with Pere Antoine at the Catholic
St. Louis Cathedral to feed, clothe, and help the poor, homeless,
and ill. She spiritually counseled prisoners and offered comfort
to them in their times of despair, and she worked tirelessly as a
nurse during many of the epidemics, including yellow fever, to
hit New Orleans. Her legacy of compassion and care for the mis-
fortunate is as great as her work as a Voodoo queen, though most
remember her for her supernatural abilities over her human
ones. There is a growing movement to have her canonized as a
saint for all of the charitable work and good deeds that she did
throughout her lifetime. Like many situations where people fear
what they don't understand, some idolized Marie while others
despised her. She was called a saint by some and a witch by others, depending on whether the person was in her good graces.

According to sources, Marie Laveau was so famous that
when she died, her obituary ran in *The New York Times*. She

was a legend, and while many good priestesses have followed in her steps, she will forever be remembered as the Voodoo queen of New Orleans.

If Marie Laveau is the official queen of Voodoo in New Orleans, the official Voodoo doctor of New Orleans would have to be Dr. John, who was known for his Voodoo spells and potions and for his knowledge of astrology and psychic abilities. Dr. John provided remedies for all types of ailments, and as the practice of Voodoo grew in New Orleans, many of these remedies could be procured through drugstores in the French Quarter and surrounding areas. Voodoo cures, as well as the rituals surrounding them, alter and shift over time as each practitioner uses his or her unique talents and skills to tap into spirit and receive guidance on how best to prepare each concoction for individual needs.

These changes in Voodoo practices occur at the top level coming from the queen, as each new queen reviewed the practices and altered them to her personal rhythm and connection with the spirits. Voodoo doctors also created their own personal spells, rituals, and concoctions, connecting not only to their personal energy but also to the energy of the city and the people and how that energy also shifted over time. While basic cures and remedies were sold in drugstores, those who sought out a strong cure of the serious nature knew to seek out a good Voodoo doctor to tend directly to their personal situations. This is still the case today, as Voodoo is currently experiencing a rebirth and is beginning to thrive again in New Orleans.

Voodoo is still a misunderstood spiritual practice. It is often confused with Hoodoo, which incorporates parts of Voodoo but also includes European folk magic practices. Hoodoo is practiced throughout most of the southern United States, particularly in the Southeast, including Louisiana, Georgia, Florida, North and South Carolina, Tennessee, Arkansas, and Alabama.

The New Orleans Historic Voodoo Museum shares the story of
Marie Laveau, the legendary Voodoo queen of New Orleans, and
offers tours to her tomb.

Hoodoo is based on magical folk practices that may incor-
porate a variety of different spiritual beliefs. Hoodoo does not
have a hierarchy attached to it, such as the Voodoo system of
a high priestess or queen. Many Hoodoo practitioners are soli-
tary in nature, rather than gathering in large groups such as in
Voodoo. Hoodoo practices are described as folk remedies, and a
great deal of the focus is based on tapping into one's individual
connection with the divine. Many describe Hoodoo as being a
variation of witchcraft with a focus on potions and cures.

Some of the most commercial variations of Hoodoo folk
remedies include the Four Thieves vinegar solution and Florida Water used in spells and concoctions. Hoodoo practitioners tend to write down their spells and recipes to pass down,
similar to the Book of Spells shared in the European witchcraft
traditions, so that tried-and-true cures can be used by future

generations. Hoodoo is actively practiced in New Orleans, and a casual observer may at first not be able to tell the difference between Hoodoo and Voodoo.

I come from a family line of practicing Hoodoo spiritual rituals and have the highest respect for them in their many forms. My great-grandmother was of French and Scottish descent, and she employed a variety of folk remedies and practices from the Hoodoo practice. She supported her family and made her living by reading tea leaves for clients in Louisiana.

 KALA'S TRAVEL TIPS

- **Visit Marie Laveau's tomb at St. Louis Cemetery #1** with a tour guide during the day. Ask for Marie to provide divine intervention to make your wish come true, but don't deface her tomb with an x. If you really want to garner her attention and get in her good graces, perform a generous act of kindness in her name after asking her to grant your wish. Make a donation in her name or help someone out in some way with no thought of reciprocation. She'll be more pleased with this act of compassion and generosity than any other type of offering.

- There are a variety of Voodoo museums to visit while in New Orleans. One of my favorites is the **New Orleans Historic Voodoo Museum** at 724 Dumaine Street. They offer tours throughout the French Quarter, including a visit to Marie's tomb.

- Spectral sightings of Marie Laveau are reported **between the 1000 and 1100 block area of St. Ann Street.** The legends state that should you see Marie, you will have good luck for the next two weeks. Marie's spirit is also reported to appear at **St. John's Voodoo Festival** each year, where she blesses all who attend the event.

- **Marie Laveau's House of Voodoo** on Bourbon Street offers talismans and psychic readings. Several years ago I had a reading here by a gentlemen who was very good. As soon as I sat down, he began to describe some of the ancient esoteric Egyptian practices that I work with in great detail—rituals that are known by very few people. I had walked in off the street looking like a tourist and had not given him my name, so he was not prepared in any way for the reading. As a psychic myself, I have found that it is very difficult for other psychics to read for me; however, this man was excellent and provided some interesting information.

- Treat yourself and **buy a Voodoo doll and a gris-gris bag** as a souvenir while visiting. Though these are not the real deal in the souvenir stores on Bourbon Street, they are colorful and delightful, and having one at your office back home is sure to be a conversation starter.

- Women in New Orleans, including Marie Laveau and the Baroness Pontalba, owned property in the city due to the colonial civil law established in Europe. Elsewhere in the United States, women could not own property until the 20th century. Many women in New Orleans were financially independent well beyond women in other parts of the country. **Women owned and operated businesses,** including clothing stores, jewelry stores, dressmaking, hair salons, bars, and, at times, brothels.

- **Bayou St. John** and the area known as **City Park** are two of the most powerful magical areas in the city. Live oaks growing around this area are very old; if you have any history of being a druid in a past life, you will resonate with the power stored in these trees.

- Voodoo doctors often purchased and sold their wares in the apothecary stores of their time in New Orleans. Creole apothecary owners were also known to make some interesting mixes and cures of their own as well. One such apothecary was **Antoine Peychaud,** who mixed bitters with brandy, sugar, and water to "bring comfort and cure the anxiety" of his customers. His secret brand of bitters made from an old family recipe quickly became a hit, and bartenders began purchasing his bitters and serving them with his prescribed amount of sugar, water, and brandy at their taverns. This concoction, known as the **Sazerac,** became the first mixed drink in New Orleans. You can still order this drink today in most of the bars in the French Quarter.

- **Florida Water** is used for spiritual blessings and cleansings for both the home and the person. It is citrus-based cologne with an orange scent that can be splashed on the body or diluted with water to use in cleaning around the home. **Four Thieves vinegar solution** is a combination of vinegars with herbs and spices that is believed to ward off the plague. It has been used since the Middle Ages.

CHAPTER 6

The Haunted Archway and Other Legends of Congo Square

"The minute you land in New Orleans, something wet and dark leaps on you and starts humping you like a swamp dog in heat, and the only way to get the aspect of New Orleans off you is to eat it off. That means beignets and crayfish bisque and jambalaya; it means shrimp remoulade, pecan pie, and red beans with rice; it means elegant pompano au papillote, funky file z'herbes, and raw oysters by the dozen; it means grillades for breakfast, a po' boy with chowchow at bedtime, and tubs of gumbo in between. It is not unusual for a visitor to the city to gain fifteen pounds in a week, yet the alternative is a whole lot worse. If you don't eat day and night, if you don't constantly funnel the indigenous flavors into your bloodstream, then the mystery beast will go right on humping you, and you will feel its sordid presence rubbing against you long after you have left town."

—Tom Robbins, *Jitterbug Perfume*

IN THE NEIGHBORHOOD OF TREME, near Rampart and Canal Streets, lies Congo Square, located inside Louis Armstrong Park. Congo Square was first established in the 1700s as a place for the enslaved people in the city to gather on Sundays, where they socialized, played music, danced with abandon, chanted, sang, and created a market space to sell their wares. The market was especially important, as some of the slaves made enough money through the sale of their crafted goods to eventually buy their freedom. It appears that this was the only park of its kind in the United States that had been established for social activity during the period of American history when there was an active slave trade.

This piece of history is surprising for many people, as throughout most of the country, enslaved people were chained up and unable to ever leave the property where they were imprisoned. In New Orleans, like most everything else culturally in the city, things were handled somewhat differently. Slaves went to the markets to shop for food and other goods throughout the week and ran errands of all types on their own. There were different types of slaves along with free people of color living in the city, and some free people of color had slaves of their own. Stringent French laws were in place in the city regarding the treatment of slaves, and people were prosecuted if they were found to be abusive and had broken these laws.

While this difference is historically noted, it is still revolting and distressing that America ever went down this horrible road at all. There is so much that could be written on the intolerable subject of slavery, and certainly many books have attempted to document the history of this time. For the purpose of this book, the focus is to attempt to describe the beauty, the testimony, and the spirit of Congo Square, which portrays the incredible strength, fortitude, and perseverance of the African people who never allowed these adversities to overcome their powerful spirit and pride.

On Sundays, Congo Square was the most happenin' and rockin' place in the city. The drums could be heard for miles, and they were mesmerizing in nature. It was said that it was hard to hear the drums and not want your body to move in tune with their rhythm. People visiting New Orleans from around the world would make plans to be at Congo Square on Sundays to hear the music and observe the elaborate dancing. Elsewhere in the United States, Protestant slave owners forbid their

The sunburst pattern entrance to Louis Armstrong Park

slaves from playing their music, which they considered heathen and unholy. Congo Square was the only place in the country where the African people were able to express themselves in their native culture. New Orleans was still operating under the French style of living, which included most of the city being Catholic, which was more lenient in this regard than the uptight Protestant colonists in the other states who had come from England. In the Catholic religion, saints are revered, and the gods from the African religion meshed very well in description with the Catholic saints, so it was seen as different expressions of the same conversation. Catholics were also more open to drinking, dancing, and celebrating than their Protestant neighbors, especially in New Orleans.

The scenes at Congo Square have been described by thousands of observers who have watched more than 500 performing dancers decorated in ribbons, shells, bones, feathers, and

Congo Square has hauntingly beautiful energy.

decorative clothing. Many of the dancers formed groups and showcased the different cultural moves and styles from the various parts of not just Africa but also the Caribbean islands, including Haiti. This custom grew each year with the music evolving, the instruments improving, and the dances becoming more elaborate until around the mid 1850s, when New Orleans became more Americanized and less French, and it was frowned upon to see this display of pure sexuality and wild abandon.

The energy and vibe of the area spilled into the streets each week. The area, surrounded by beautiful oaks and the lush nature of Louisiana, held court with the dancers and musicians in a cadence of pleasure, spiritual renewal, and communion with nature and the gods. Reportedly there were many Voodoo practitioners in attendance who were able to skillfully work their magic and rituals into the dancing, keeping it a secret from those who were not in the know. This allowed the community to celebrate their sacred practices and pray to their gods, thereby keeping their faith alive. In this sacred area, the gods heard the calls of their people and they responded, blessing them with some of the most incredible soul-stirring music that the world has ever known. The sounds reverberated in the air, waking the spirits from the ancient oak trees and the elementals of nature, stirring energy for freedom—freedom of expression, freedom from misery, and, most important, freedom from oppression. It also emerged as a birthplace for the musical heritage in New Orleans, and the spirits can still be heard, called upon, and felt by those who live in the Treme area.

After the Civil War, Congo Square continued to be a gathering place, especially for musicians, and is considered to be one of the traditional areas, along with Storyville, where the musicality of jazz began. Congo Square now features statues of famous musicians, including Louis Armstrong.

As you enter the square from North Rampart Street, you walk through a large archway with triangular points in the arch resembling a half sunrise. The spirits still wander through Congo Square as decades of music and prayer have called them into being at this location. Many locals share their stories of having prayed to these spirits, asking them for favors while in the park.

It appears that due to this archway being built, this connection has been strengthened in ways that were not understood by the officials who built the structure. Any practitioner of the old sacred ways is aware of the tween spaces, which creates a portal that connects with the other worlds. Gates and doorways are tween places, and the most magical times to connect with the spirit world are during the tween times between light and dark, also known as sunrise and sunset.

Building an archway on this legendary sacred ground created a tween space, allowing those who seek to speak with spirits a significant opportunity. Many people have reported experiencing supernatural events when nearing the gate and immediately after walking through it. It is no surprise that a gate of this size, which was built in the shape of the sun rising from the ground, would activate the spiritual energy generated on this ground for decades. The energy is further heightened as musicians continue to play here in the park.

The gate is very life-affirming to me, and I see it as a positive sign for the rebirth and renewal of New Orleans, calling forth the ancient gods to come through and see the city through troubled times as it continues to rebuild after Hurricane Katrina.

When visiting Congo Square, I had a past life déjà vu experience. I remembered living in New Orleans in another lifetime and watching the people dance while my mother pulled me away from the scene. Oh how I cried, wanting to be with them. I was quite young, and I felt the music ripple through my entire body, making me want to dance. I was one with the drums and the dancing, and I longed to surrender to the feeling. Dancing to this day is still like this for me; I feel it in my soul to the tips of my toes, and it transcends me from time and space into another realm.

On another visit to New Orleans, my husband and I took a carriage ride one evening on what we thought would be a nice romantic adventure. We asked our guide to show us some of the areas that we had not seen recently, and we ventured further into this area of the city near Congo Square. As we wandered through the streets in the carriage, night fell quickly and the energy of the city changed as streetlamps highlighted the darkened roads. We were enjoying our time in the carriage and were quite relaxed until I felt a cold chill crawling over my body. The chill was not coming from the air, but rather being sent psychically by someone. I bolted upright out of my husband's arms, immediately alarmed by this invasive energy blast.

Looking around, I began to scan the area to determine where the source of this energy was coming from, as it was palatable, sinister, and very strong. My husband realized that something was wrong, and at the same time, the driver of our carriage began having trouble controlling the mule, who had become very agitated.

The cold forbidding energy continued to crawl across me, like a dark fog that chilled me from the inside out. I had never felt such a controlling energy from any type of supernatural being like this before. The most shocking part was the mental hypnotic suggestion it was able to send, telling me there was nowhere to run, nowhere to go, and that I should sit quietly, as he would be here soon.

Ignoring this mental suggestion, I said to the driver, "We need to get out of here now!" while he was struggling with the mule who was doing his best to turn the carriage around himself, against the driver's wishes.

I instructed the driver to let the mule go the direction he wanted to go and to allow him to move as quickly as he could, as the tour was now over. Relieved by my statement, the driver seemed to snap out of his hypnotic stage and relaxed his grip on the reins. The mule took over from there, turning the carriage around in the street and moving as quickly as I have ever seen a mule move.

As the carriage turned, I honed in on the location of the entity and turned to look back at the direction we had been heading until we turned around. Standing there at the end of the street, I saw the figure of what appeared to be a man. Having recovered from the initial shock of the psychic attack, I had pulled my white light energy shield around me and used my abilities to scan him. I then sent him a "how does it feel to be scanned" blast of energy. As I scanned him, it quickly became apparent that he wasn't human. To my great surprise, it was what I discerned to be a vampire—a creature that I had only read about and never knew if it still truly existed in this day. Yet, there he stood.

Several years later, I shared this story with the legendary author and paranormal researcher Brad Steiger, while he was my guest on the *Explore Your Spirit* show. We were discussing paranormal entities and our run-ins with them over the years. I described the event in great detail to him, including how the psychic energy spread over my body with the probing mental suggestions, which attempted to lull me into a passive state as it had done with the carriage driver. Brad went on to tell me that I was indeed very fortunate to have escaped this attack, as it is rare to break free from this type of psychic hold when it is extended. I resolved after that experience to keep a shield of some sort around me at all times in order to sense any type of entity that may come in my vicinity. As for that night, we have the mule to thank, as he reacted as any animal would in the presence of something sinister. His constant pulling and agitated state helped me snap the driver out of his hypnotic state, as the driver was fully intent on continuing down this road where the vampire stood waiting at the end of the road.

I have never felt this type of energy again, and I can offer no proof of the existence of vampires beyond my personal experience, which I know to be real and authentic. From this brief encounter, I can say with conviction that vampires are not sparkly or friendly, and that Anne Rice has offered the best description of their inner nature and workings.

As I've shared this encounter with various paranormal experts, several have speculated that I encountered the vampire known as Jacques St. Germaine, who lived at the corner of Ursuline and Royal Streets in the French Quarter in 1902. The legend states that he is a descendant of Count St. Germaine, who has the reputation of being immortal. Jacques moved from France to New Orleans, and shortly after his arrival in NOLA, police began to suspect him of criminal activity after several women were reported missing after being seen with him. After one woman jumped from a second-floor balcony at his home, police were called in. She gave the statement that he was a vampire and that he had tried to attack and feed from her. His friends told police that the woman was drunk and that Jacques would come to the police station in the morning to give a full statement of the evening's activities.

The next morning Jacques had disappeared. When police searched his home they found no food, nor any dining or cooking utensils, with the exception of wineglasses with red liquid inside, which was found to be a mixture of blood and wine. They also found piles of tablecloths stained with blood, with some stains more recent than others. Reportedly, Jacques returned back to New Orleans a decade later, where he resumed his activities and has remained in the city ever since. According to the sources in the city that I spoke with about my experience, the description of the manner, demeanor, and style of vampire that I encountered has convinced them that it was Jacques St. Germaine whom I encountered on the street in New Orleans. They also shared that it is rare to escape his clutches and that I have a strong will and presence of mind to have done so in such a close encounter.

⚜ Kala's Travel Tips

- Take the **carriage ride** and ask your driver to deviate from his normal route and show you Congo Square, along with some other sights that aren't typically part of the tour. You'll see more of New Orleans this way, and they may enjoy the break from the same route as well. Most carriage drivers have a wealth of knowledge about the city and its history and are happy to share this information. I recommend this for day excursions, so you avoid my night experience in the carriage. Crime also has become more of a problem in this area, so it's not a good area to travel at night.

- The **Mahalia Jackson Theater for the Performing Arts** is located here with fine performances available to attend all year.

- If you are daring while entering through the gates of Louis Armstrong Park, **touch the archway** and ask the spirits to send you a message. Be respectful while doing so and be warned, for they are strong and powerful. Don't ask if you aren't prepared to receive whatever message they bring.

- If at all possible, visit this area during **Jazz Fest,** where the dead and everyone else in New Orleans come alive with the music.

CHAPTER 7

The Horrors Still Live at LaLaurie House

"Death is not the greatest loss in life. The greatest loss is what dies inside us while we live."

—Norman Cousins

FILLED WITHIN THE PAGES of every haunted book are sinister, macabre, and bloodcurdling anecdotes based on love lost and tarnished with bitter memories. As you delve deeper, you soon happen upon the one story that raises the creepiness factor to a whole new level. This tale is always told in a hushed tone, with the storyteller looking over his or her shoulder to make sure that the wrong person doesn't overhear what is about to be shared. As the story unfolds, the tale is so bizarre and horrific that, as the words spill across the page, a deep chill builds within you until it slowly runs downs your spine. Somewhere deep inside, you know that you truly don't want to hear this story, yet you find yourself leaning forward in your seat to ensure you don't missing hearing a single word.

This story is one of those dark and hideous ventures, so sit back, dim the lights, and think twice before venturing further into this twisted tale. *You've been warned.*

Marie Delphine LaLaurie, or Madame LaLaurie as she was called, was a prominent figurehead in New Orleans society, coming from a family that had done well both financially and politically. Wealthy, beautiful, and established, she lived in one of the most beautiful homes in the French Quarter of New Orleans. Now on her third marriage, she had married

Dr. Leonard Louis Nicolas LaLaurie, a doctor who was a great deal younger than his wife. Marie, along with her two daughters from a previous marriage, settled into their new home with Dr. LaLaurie at 1140 Royal Street and looked forward to her new social status as a doctor's wife.

Madame Marie's home was decorated with priceless antiques and works of art, and her social calendar was full of party invitations and formal dinners throughout the year. Like most of the wealthy social classes living in the city at this time, she maintained her home through the use of enslaved people as servants. While this was a common act in New Orleans at the time, her treatment of the servants was highly unusual according to neighbors and others in the community. The lack of care and attention to her servants became the topic of gossip throughout the quarter, as well as the manner in which they were kept locked inside the home.

On Sundays in New Orleans, slaves were allowed to congregate at Congo Square, where they danced and socialized. While almost all of the enslaved people gathered there each Sunday, Madame LaLaurie's servants were never allowed to attend the festivities. During the few instances when they were seen publicly, they were described to be in poor health, their bodies thin and haggard with an overall sickly appearance. Each time one of her servants was seen looking ill, the rumors would fly, yet they would be quickly dismissed as others were quick to point out that Madame LaLaurie had recently freed two of her slaves and helped them with financial means to begin their new life.

Certain rumors continued to spread about Madame LaLaurie's slaves by one of the neighbors. It was said that she chained her cook to the kitchen stove and kept her there all day while Madame LaLaurie starved the slaves for days. The rumors grew over time, stating that she had beat her two daughters severely when she caught them sneaking food to the starving slaves.

Beautiful architectural view of the LaLaurie home

One day, shouting was heard coming from the LaLaurie mansion, which led to the same neighbor reporting the incident to the police. The neighbor reported glimpsing through open windows at the LaLaurie home to see Madame chasing one of her young servants through the house with a whip. Reportedly, the young girl ran screaming up the stairs until she reached the top floor. She then climbed out on the roof to escape the lashes of the whip. While on the roof, she lost her footing and fell to her death.

An investigation was called forth based on the neighbor's report. Local gossips reported that the LaLauries were mistreating their slaves, which was a criminal offense in New Orleans. Unlike other parts of the country, which ran under the Puritan/British rule for treatment of slaves, Louisiana operated under the Code Noir from the French colonial rule, which gave some protection to slaves, including forbidding any type of torture and abuse.

After the investigation of the incident with the young girl falling from the roof, the slaves were ordered to be removed from the home and sold at auction. The story continues that Madame, having significant pull in the community, called in some favors and instructed her friends and family to purchase the slaves at auction and quietly return them to her home the next evening.

Once this story entered the rumor mill, people began to pick sides as to whether they believed Madame or the neighbor. A lawyer had been sent to investigate the treatment of her slaves, and he had reported finding no ill treatment of anyone at the home. Friends of Madame shared that, during the elaborate dinner parties she held, she was often seen sharing the last of her wine with her servants.

People who liked Madame dismissed the rumors as coming from the new Americans in town, who were jealous of Creole society with their elitist social standing and prominence in the city. It was viewed as jealousy and malicious gossip, as Madame was beautiful, wealthy, and charming, and this alone was enough to make people envious and want to see her brought down in some fashion. The gossip ran back and forth but never amounted to anything deeper.

Madame's life continued on as normal until April 10, 1834, when the elderly cook reportedly chained to the stove in the kitchen set fire to the house. Knowing she would perish with this act, as there was no escape from her chains, it was speculated that she would rather die a horrific death by being burned alive rather than live another day in servitude. Some of the gossips stated that the young girl who had fallen to her death in the courtyard was the granddaughter of the cook, and that, overcome with grief from her granddaughter's death, the cook could no longer stand to be in the home.

As the fire began to spread through the house, alarms were sounded to bring the firemen. Observers reported that Madame remained calm during the fire, instructing slaves and neighbors who had arrived to carry the antiques and paintings safely out of harm's way. One of the neighbors who pitched in to help was Judge Canongo. The judge later reported that he had asked Madame's husband, Dr. LaLaurie, where the other slaves were located and that Dr. LaLaurie had replied something along the lines: "Never mind the slaves. Mind your own business and get back to the task at hand."

What happened next during this melee shocked the city of New Orleans. One of the neighbors shouted to the others that some of the slaves were locked up inside the attic. Rescue workers and firemen rushed up the stairs to the attic door, only to find it bolted and locked shut. Using pickaxes, they broke open the door and were greeted by a putrid smell accompanied by a sea of festering bodies in various states of decay.

Some of the slaves were chained to walls, while others were locked inside cages around the room. They had been starved nearly to death as well as seriously abused and horrifically mutilated. Body parts lay in various states of decomposition around the room, and a roughly staged surgical area held instruments that had been used on the men and women.

Reports of the crude surgeries performed on these people included sex change operations and lobotomies where the holes remained open to the brain and maggots were seen moving inside. On other people, their bones had been broken and reset in an attempt to arrange the human body to look animalistic in the shapes of crabs and other bizarre forms. Some were trapped in iron neck braces and chained upside down while others had their eyes gouged out and strips of skin removed from various parts of their body.

Almost all of the slaves were near death, and, for many, it appeared this would be a kinder fate. The rescue workers were overwhelmed with the stench of human waste, as well as the gruesome and terrifying sights before them. They worked as quickly as possible to unshackle the men and women and carry them out of the home before the fire reached this level. Some of them were so ill and weak that they died in the rescue workers' arms while being transported out of the home. Those who survived the ordeal were taken to the nearby Cabildo building to be quickly treated by medical professionals.

According to the legend, an angry mob, shocked and disgusted by this news, began to spread the word throughout the city that the rumors and gossip for years about how the servants were treated at the LaLaurie home were true. The mob grew in size and returned back to the LaLaurie house after hearing that the slaves were being cared for at the Cabildo.

As the mob approached the LaLaurie home, they began to tear at the front door and break the windows. They reportedly poured into the home, destroying everything in sight. In the midst of this destruction, Madame LaLaurie burst through the side gate in her carriage with her driver at the helm. She escaped by racing at breakneck speed through the streets until she reached the docks, where a boat was waiting to carry her away.

It was reported that her daughters had escaped earlier by passing undetected through a neighbor's home, and that her husband had slipped away earlier to meet her at the arranged rendezvous. Some of the mob chased after the carriage, hoping to catch her, while the rest of the group tore apart the house and looted the rest of the belongings in the home. It was said that the people were close to breaking apart the banisters to the stairs and preparing to tear down the walls when the police appeared and took control, dispersing the group and sending them home.

Police patrolled the house for almost a month afterward to keep looters and angry mobs from completely destroying the home. Several of the officers were said to have reported hearing

Ornate entrance to the LaLaurie home

scratching sounds and strange shrieks and moans coming from within the home late at night, and word began to spread that the house was haunted.

From this point onward, the house has been considered to be under a dark curse. All future attempts to use the home in one form or another have ended badly. It has been used as a school for girls, which closed suddenly due to rumors of scandals by the teachers, leading to the girls being quickly removed from the school for protection. It also functioned as a music academy, which was closed due to a similar scandal with children. The home also operated as a bar, housing for Italian immigrants, and a private residence. None of these solutions lasted for long, as all of the residents or patrons reported experiencing feelings of dread, gloom, and despair, as well as experiencing haunted activity, including screams, rustling of chains, loud shrieks, and the sounds of people moving and writhing in pain in the attic.

One of the most interesting reports of supernatural activity reported at the home comes from the 1950s, when the home operated as a furniture store. The store owner began to complain that someone was breaking into the store each night and putting a gooey and foul-smelling liquid all over the furniture. He was so upset by the destruction of his furniture that he decided to stay overnight in the store with a shotgun, ready to shoot the vandals who were entering the store.

He stayed up as long as he could and drifted off to sleep for only a few minutes before waking to find the sticky substance on the furniture with no signs of entry into the building. From the descriptions he provided, paranormal researchers today would refer to this substance as ectoplasm. The paranormal activity continued nightly in the store, and the owner was forced to close down the business and move elsewhere to preserve his inventory.

In 2007, actor Nicholas Cage purchased the home, only to be forced to put it back on the market a year later. In the fall of 2011 during my visit to New Orleans, I walked past the home to see that it was undergoing a deep renovation. A corporation had purchased the home, and almost everyone in town whom I spoke with had an opinion about what was going on inside. Most residents speculated that it was going to be turned into apartment-style residences that would be sold individually. A shudder passed through me on hearing this news, as it's difficult to imagine that time has healed the wounds in this house. It seems to be only resting until a new unsuspecting victim arrives on the scene. Yet I couldn't be sure that these stories were real. Were they merely rumors and legends that had grown over time and been embellished as many ghost stories are? All I could do here was stand outside the home in the daylight, watching construction workers hammering and moving supplies in and out. The house looked lovely. The architecture of this home is gorgeous, and I can only imagine that great detail is being taken inside to continue the look and feel of the home. How did it have this beautiful facade if it had been ripped down to its foundation inside and out by mobs of people?

Maybe it was just too chaotic by day for me to feel anything deeper, or maybe the stories are just that, truly eerie ghosts stories that built on each detail over time. With that thought in mind, I decided to move past the local legends and tales and do some deeper investigating.

For well over a century, this is where the tale of the LaLaurie house had ended, leaving the reputation of Madame scarred beyond belief and only a horrendous tale of misery and incredible pain attached to the home on this block of Royal Street. Yet as I did more digging into the home, it appears that more information has come to light, and there is much more to the story.

In a new book titled *Mad Madame LaLaurie*, authors Victoria Love and Lorelei Shannon decided to delve deeper into the story and move past the rumors, speculation, and sensationalism of this tale to see what truly occurred in this home. What they discovered is that when one begins to research the story to confirm the legend, most of the reported facts quickly fall apart. The story became so terrifying that the rumors continued to grow each decade, becoming wilder and more sensational.

The gossip first began with rumors that Madame, who was always beautifully coiffed and dressed, would throw elaborate parties at her home. It was said that during these parties, she would excuse herself for 15 minutes and retire upstairs. Reportedly, she was so bloodthirsty that she would take this break to go upstairs and whip her servants, spilling their blood and watching with glee as the blood flew around the room and splattered the walls.

When the witnesses were later questioned and asked if this was truly what they had experienced during the parties that they reportedly attended at her home, several of them stated that this was indeed the truth. These witnesses were then asked how Madame was able to return downstairs in the same clothes she had worn all evening with no blood found on her clothing, nor looking disheveled in the least, including her perfectly coiffed hair; to this they had no reliable answer. When these witnesses were asked to describe what the home looked like inside and to give names of other guests who had attended the same dinner party, they could not give accurate descriptions of the home nor identify anyone else at the dinner party.

Investigators also began to wonder why Madame was the one blamed for the events that supposedly went on in the home. A deeper look into the witness testimony showed that the people who were the quickest to testify against Madame were people who were reportedly jealous of her for one reason or another, whether it was her beauty, her social standing, or her wealth. None of the witnesses had ever actually seen her mistreat anyone in any manner. They were only reporting what they had heard from local gossip, which all began from one neighbor.

The neighbor's statement about seeing Madame whipping a young girl until she fell to her death also appears to be false. The neighbor said that he had witnessed the young girl being buried in the dirt near the courtyard, and that several other bodies would be found there, which also had been buried at night to cover up their deaths. A moment of common sense sees right through this testimony, as how many people can you imagine would watch someone fall to his or her death and then wait until the body was buried in the courtyard before reaching out to the police. This neighbor also testified that other bodies were buried in the same location, implying that he had watched this scene several times, yet never reported it as a crime to the authorities.

Conflicting statements later surfaced stating that there was never a young girl who had been whipped and chased by Madame from the rooftop, but rather a young slave boy had crawled up on the rooftop on his own and had slipped, falling to his death. These statements, when investigated further, found that these testimonies again had no eyewitness reports and were stories told by a friend of a friend of a friend and had been passed along the rumor mill.

As researchers looked at the official investigation report, it stated that the entire courtyard area had been dug up by the police, and no bones or bodies were ever discovered. It was never proven that this incident occurred. Further investigations of court records incredulously show that there were no legal prosecutions against Madame during this investigation. It is now believed that the stories of her slaves being removed from the home after the reports of cruelty were completely fabricated.

It appears that some people were so intent upon incriminating Madame that they pinned all sorts of sinister activities against her. Yet when looking at the official public records in the city, what they show is that Madame freed two slaves of her own and helped them financially as well. Other legal records show that she petitioned for a legal separation from Dr. LaLaurie and reported that the reason for her request of separation was due to spousal abuse. She swore on oath that he was beating and wounding her in unmentionable manners and pleaded to be released from her marriage to him.

Oddly enough, through all of these records and tales, most people know very little about Dr. LaLaurie. He was known to be an antisocial person who preferred to stay occupied with his surgical work, which was done inside the home.

Here in public records, we have Madame reporting being abused by him and asking to be legally separated from him. When the fire broke out in the home and the slaves were found, they reportedly had experienced the most bizarre surgeries of all kinds. Why was the attention and investigation not turned to Dr. LaLaurie, a surgeon, who would certainly be capable of these types of atrocities? The records state that Dr. LaLaurie was a surgeon who specialized in physical deformities and had been known for operating on hunchbacks in France to correct their skeletal structure.

The stories of Madame, Dr. LaLaurie, and the children conspiring to escape together after the fire also appear to be fabricated. When Madame ran for her life after the fire, some say she escaped to Paris while other members of her family stayed behind in New Orleans.

Dr. LaLaurie, on the other hand, departed quietly from the scene and disappeared, never to be seen again with Madame or anyone else related to the family. There was also the judge's testimony that when he questioned Dr. LaLaurie about the location of the slaves, the doctor had deliberately tried to stop him from finding and freeing the slaves.

What if all this time, Dr. Louis LaLaurie had been abusing Madame and her two daughters, and threatening her life and her children's lives while he conducted horrific torturous experiments in the attic?

There is little known about Dr. LaLaurie personally before his marriage to Madame. In most cases of sadistic behavior, signs of mental instability are typically revealed early on in the person's life. While no one knew the childhood history of Dr. Louis LaLaurie before he moved to New Orleans, most of the city had known Madame Marie since she was a little girl. She had never shown any acts of cruelty throughout her life, and her first two marriages were completely without rumor or trouble with her servants of any kind.

She was well regarded by many in the city and had been known to free some of her servants as well as to have loaned money to a free woman of color who wanted to start her own business. In comparison to her husband, the surgeon, who was a newcomer in town and kept to himself, did she become another victim of his cruelty, first through cruel physical abuse and then by receiving the blame for his dastardly deeds while he escaped scot-free?

Madame spent the rest of her life labeled as a monster. Some say she lived in Paris while longing to return to live in New Orleans, missing her family and her life there in the only city she called home. Other reports say that she never left the area and lived nearby in the city once the event settled down. Years later it was reportedly learned that the neighbor who started all of the malicious gossip and rumors was actually a former business partner of her deceased brother's who was trying to discredit Madame and gain control of her assets. His rumors were fueled by yellow journalism and the love of shocking stories and gossip in the city.

Madame is buried in St. Louis Cemetery #1. It is difficult to imagine her soul at rest, as she continues to be blamed and despised by those who call her the most sadistic and cruel woman in New Orleans. If this were the case, it would be easy to assume that her tortured soul still roams the streets of New Orleans, looking for Dr. LaLaurie and the gossipy neighbor to finally settle the score with both of them.

The last form of communication received from Dr. LaLaurie was a letter he wrote to a family member stating that he was living in Cuba. He had written to inquire if the family member would ship his medical instruments to him from New Orleans to Cuba. A date of death and burial location is unknown for Dr. LaLaurie, and the mystery of his whereabouts continue to this day. In retrospect, it certainly appears that the surgical monstrosities performed on these people were more likely to have been achieved by a surgeon rather than a Creole high-society lady of leisure.

I went back again to visit the LaLaurie home and peered through the windows. The windows were uncovered, and the view inside only showed the various stages of construction and renovation. I could only stand outside the home along the sidewalk, as it is privately owned and not open to the public. Several ghost researchers report that if one stands on the corner at night, ghosts can be seen through the upstairs windows. During the time I visited, the upstairs windows were boarded up with plywood and no ghosts were around to be seen.

The house is quite striking, and several people walked by while I was there. I was standing next to the house and had placed my hand on the outside wall to see if I could psychically tap into the energy of the home. Watching me for a moment, the people walking by stopped and asked me in a hushed tone, "Is this the house? Is this the haunted LaLaurie house?" When I replied that indeed it was, they shivered, laughed nervously, and quickly moved back from the building to stand in the street. A group of workmen were coming out of the home at this point with materials, and there was just too much activity on the street for me to spend much time there in quiet concentration. A tour carriage also had pulled up, and the tour guide was asking me if I had seen any ghosts at the house. Tourists began snapping photos of me standing outside the house as if I was part of the tour. I replied that I had not seen any ghosts at this point in time, and I ended my investigation, as it was proving to be too distracting outside to attempt to communicate with any of the entities inside without entry into the home.

Perhaps the best person to report if haunted activity is still ongoing within the home would be its former owner, actor Nicholas Cage.

Kala's Travel Tips

- If you've seen the TV show *American Horror Story,* this home could give that house a run for its money. More horrific activities have occurred at this home over the years, and no one has ever been able to rest easy in the home. The house appears to have a presence, an entity that has developed from all the torture and misery experienced in the home. The entity seems to have an effect on all who stay in the home, leading many of them to do dark deeds of their own.

- One of the most intriguing stories ever reported in regards to Dr. and Madame LaLaurie was that a woman in the city had visited the swamps where she had sex with a demon and later gave birth to what is described as a **devil baby.** The woman reportedly turned the baby over to Marie Laveau to handle the situation. It was reported that Marie Laveau was friends with Madame LaLaurie and had delivered the devil baby to Dr. and Madame LaLaurie to raise. No other mention of this devil child, reported to be both physically deformed and mentally insane, was ever heard again until it was said that the child died at the age of 5. Most people discount this story, saying that Marie Laveau had a good heart and may have helped care for this child and, knowing Madame, asked for her to offer assistance of some sort with the child, who was most likely suffering from a terrible physical deformity.

- **Is the LaLaurie House the most haunted building in New Orleans?** Without having the opportunity to go inside the building, I truly can't say yay or nay at this point. During your next visit to the city, stand on the corner and look to see if ghosts appear at the window or if you hear strange moans and groans.

- Reportedly, the last owner, Nicholas Cage, experienced some financial difficulties, and the home went up for sale via auction, lending more credibility to the **curse** that befalls anyone who owns the home.

- While I was in New Orleans investigating this story, a local magazine ran a story by Emily Hingle, who provided extremely **helpful details regarding the research of Madame LaLaurie.** She reports that in 1934, *The Times-Picayune* reported that Madame was not to blame for what occurred. The reporter in 1934, Meigs Frost, revealed that the neighbor who had told the firemen that slaves were chained in the attic was a Monsieur Montreuil. It turns out that Montreuil was a beneficiary of the estate of L. B. Macarty, who was Madame's brother, and Madame was the administrator of her brother's estate. The reporter found numerous legal challenges and notices posted in the newspapers during 1840 through 1850, all of which Madame won against Montreuil. It is now suspected that Montreuil started all of these rumors to cast suspicion on her and to ruin her reputation. Hingle reports that Frost also uncovered that Madame continued to have court documents regarding property disputes listed after leaving the house on Royal Street, and there appears to be growing evidence that she never went to Paris and instead moved to the Treme area of New Orleans.

CHAPTER 8

The Casket Girls of Ursuline Convent and Other Vampire Lore

"There are such beings as vampires, some of us have evidence that they exist. Even had we not the proof of our own unhappy experience, the teachings and the records of the past give proof enough for sane peoples."

—Bram Stoker, *Dracula*

THE URSULINE CONVENT was built for a small group of nuns who organized the convent into an orphanage, school, and hospital, making this the oldest school for girls in America. The nuns were brave and tough. They had left France under very troubled times and were now braving the New World during political turmoil. Louisiana was bouncing back and forth between multiple countries, and each change brought new rules and policies that also affected the religious organizations in the city.

The French Revolution had caused great turmoil, and Pope Pius VII had been placed under arrest in Rome by Napoleon. As ownership of Louisiana changed often, the sisters were concerned as to what their fate would be as they struggled to create a place of education, healing, and care for children. During the time that Louisiana was owned by the Spanish, nuns from Spain had come to the convent to assist with the work there. Later, during the revolution, France took back control of Louisiana, causing the Spanish nuns to fear for their safety. Many of the nuns fled to Cuba, leaving only a small group of sisters to run the school.

It is said that from the beginning of Ursuline, miracles were seen at this convent under the blessing of the Virgin Mary. Over the years, the nuns had worked tirelessly to build the school. They had lost many of their sisters due to political conflicts, were struggling, and were short on help. When their leader, Mother St. Xavier Farjon, passed away in 1810, things appeared very bleak as the future seemed very shaky and unsure for Ursuline.

One of the sisters wrote to her cousin, Mother St. Michel Gensoul, in France, asking her to heed the call for help and come as soon as possible to assist in running Ursuline. Moving to New Orleans was a big change from life in Europe, and Mother St. Michel prayed for guidance and enlightenment on what she should do. She received the answer through her prayers that she should make the journey to New Orleans to help the sisters of Ursuline.

When Mother St. Michel spoke to the bishop to ask his permission to travel to New Orleans, he did not want her to leave because help was also shorthanded in France after the revolution. The bishop didn't want to be responsible for directly telling her no, so he told her that in order for her to leave, she would need written permission from the pope. This was impossible at the time, as the pope had been imprisoned by Napoleon, and the guards were under strict instructions to stop any letters from being received or sent out.

This information did not deter Mother St. Michel from her task. Instead, it only strengthened her conviction and prayers. Knowing that anything is possible when the Blessed Mother Mary wants her divine will to be done, Mother St. Michel began to pray to Mary, asking her to intercede on her behalf so that she could help the sisters of Ursuline.

The Old Ursuline Convent

Up until this time, Mary was referred to as the Virgin Mary, the Blessed Mother Mary, or Our Lady of Perpetual Aid. Because the nun needed a miracle to happen so quickly to receive permission to help the nuns of Ursuline, Mother St. Michel said in her prayers that if Mary interceded on her behalf, she would establish the Blessed Mother's name in New Orleans as Our Lady of Prompt Succor (Quick Aid) in honor of her assistance. Mother St. Michel wrote her letter to the pope and mailed it off, having full faith that a miracle would occur and the letter would reach the pope against all odds.

Slightly less than a month later, a letter arrived to Mother St. Michel in France from a cardinal in Rome. The cardinal stated that he was operating under the specific orders and instructions received directly from the pope, who had miraculously received her letter to him while imprisoned. The pope had instructed the cardinal to grant full permission for Mother to travel to Ursuline, and the bishop had to acknowledge that a miracle had occurred.

Mother St. Michel wasted no time and ordered that a statue of the Blessed Mary be carved immediately and named Our Lady of Prompt Succor. Both the statue and Mother St. Michel set sail together and arrived in New Orleans, where the statue was placed at Ursuline. Shortly thereafter, more miracles began to occur.

The first reported miracle occurred in 1812, when a devastating fire roared through New Orleans, destroying most of the city. The Great Fire grew out of control due to the high winds that day. It quickly swept over the city, destroying everything in its path, and headed directly toward Ursuline Convent.

All hope had been lost in the city, and an order was received to evacuate Ursuline at once, for imminent destruction by fire was only minutes away. Inside the convent, Sister Anthony placed a small statue of Our Lady of Prompt Succor in the window, and Mother St. Michel began to pray aloud, asking Mary to intercede again on their behalf.

According to a large number of witnesses, right after Mother St. Michel said the prayer aloud, the fire immediately shifted direction and died down, allowing itself to be extinguished. The convent was saved, making it one of only a few structures in the city to be spared by the fire. The nuns attributed this to their prayers for protection to Our Lady of Prompt Succor, and it was considered to be a miracle. Had the convent been one of the buildings destroyed by fire during this time, it is highly unlikely that funds would have been allocated to rebuild the structure; this would have ended the school, and the nuns would have returned to France or moved on to Cuba.

While this devastating loss of life, homes, and businesses rattled the city to its core, the one good thing to come from the fire was that the new architectural design led to the future preservation of the city. The Spanish rebuilt the city using stucco and brick, creating many of the structures still standing today in the French Quarter. Before the fire, most of the buildings were made from all wood structures of French design, which did not hold up well against the elements in the city.

The second great miracle occurred in 1815, when General Andrew Jackson was preparing to fight the British in the Battle of New Orleans. Things did not look good for New Orleans, as the American troops were greatly outnumbered, with more than 15,000 British troops who were highly organized and well-armed against the less organized 6,000 American troops with few supplies.

Almost everyone in New Orleans feared that the city was doomed. The gravity of the situation was enormous, for not only would the British rule the city, but they would also have control over the supplies shipped via the Mississippi River as well as the ships entering the port from the gulf. British ownership of the Port of New Orleans would severely cripple and weaken American access to resources. The loss of this battle would have far-reaching complications that went way beyond the welfare of the residents of New Orleans.

The wives, sisters, mothers, and daughters of the city decided to do the only thing they could think to do in this moment of crisis. They gathered together at the Ursuline Convent with the nuns and prayed all night long for the safety of the city, asking that the American troops would be victorious. Many of these soldiers included their husbands, sons, fathers, uncles, and brothers.

After praying all night, the women gathered together early the next morning on January 8 for Mass in front of the statue of Our Lady of Prompt Succor. The prayers were directed to the Blessed Mother Mary in her role as the Lady of Prompt Succor. The women asked Mary to intervene on behalf of their

Close-up view of the windows at the Old Ursuline Convent

prayers, expressing aloud to her that if the city was saved and the British defeated, January 8 would become a yearly feast day in her honor.

Later that evening, news arrived that the British had been miraculously defeated and New Orleans was saved. General Jackson later visited the convent to thank the nuns in person for his victory, saying that he had felt the divine intervention and blessing of their prayers. From this moment on, Our Lady of Prompt Succor has been the patron saint to watch over New Orleans.

Based on the beautiful outpouring of charity and compassion shown by the sisters of Ursuline, along with the miracles occurring at the convent, this story could end right here with enough supernatural occurrences to rival any other paranormal location in New Orleans. But like most supernatural areas where goodness dwells in the light, the shadows are soon to follow, and the darkness is sure to hover nearby.

This is where we venture into the time that darkness fell over Ursuline and supernatural beings decided to make the convent their new home.

On any haunted tour while visiting New Orleans, your guide is sure to mention the Ursuline Convent and take you to the see the building. What they won't be mentioning, though, are the above-mentioned miracles that occurred at this site. Instead they'll share with you tales of vampires and the casket girls of Ursuline. What may be the most unsettling part of this legend is that the tales are not all from the past. Rather, the vampires are still reported to be here today.

As France began their campaign to populate the new city of New Orleans, they first gathered poor women from the streets and prisons of Paris and shipped them to New Orleans to entice men to settle in the city. After exhausting this effort, their second round of recruiting women was to reach out to the French convents and invite orphaned young ladies residing at convents to make the move to New Orleans.

Each of these girls arrived from France with a trunk shaped in the form of a small casket, which had been provided to them by the French government. Inside these trunks were the belongings that each young girl would need to start her life in the new city. The term used to refer to these young girls was *fille à la cassette* ("girl with a casket") and later shortened to "casket girl."

These casket girls from the convents arrived in New Orleans, where they lived and were educated at Ursuline Convent and then introduced to society, where they would meet their future husbands. This was a normal type of courtship arrangement in these days. While this is interesting from a historical perspective, little would be spoken about this situation from a paranormal perspective all these years later, except that one day a very strange group of young ladies arrived at Ursuline Convent.

Late one evening, a group of young women arrived in New Orleans by ship, stating that they had been sent to study at Ursuline Convent. To the surprise of the men unloading their trunks from the ship, these girls did not have the typical small caskets like the other girls who arrived from France. Rather, these girls had traveled with very curious containers shaped like full-size coffins. These caskets were locked tight, and when the girls arrived at the convent, they gave strict instructions that the caskets could never be opened until the day they had left the convent to be married. When asked why, the girls replied that the caskets contained their valuable dowry.

Many other young girls had arrived at Ursuline with odd-shaped trunks that somewhat resembled coffins, and some of these did indeed contain dowries for their marriage. Yet this particular group of girls, who had arrived as a unified group, carried caskets that were much larger, heavier, and more elaborate in design. The caskets were placed on the third floor of the convent, where they were stored per the dowry instructions. This is normally where the caskets were stored for each girl upon her arrival, but what made this request unusual is that the girls usually unpacked some of the items from their casket upon their arrival at Ursuline, versus the request here that the caskets be left locked and remain untouched.

It is here that the legend begins. Late one evening, one of the sisters decided to go up to the third floor and open one of the caskets to see what was so special inside. To her surprise, the coffin was empty. As she opened the others, she discovered that they were all empty as well. She reported this to another one of the sisters, and it was feared that this particular group of casket girls had brought vampires with them over from Europe.

The decision was made to give a special blessing of protection for the convent. More than 8,000 screws were blessed and then used to seal the windows shut on the third floor. This act was done to prevent the vampires, who were at this time out of their caskets, from being able to reenter the convent before daylight to sleep in the caskets. The legend states that once the blessed screws were placed in the windows, the girls downstairs became agitated and restless in their sleep. Later that evening a howl was heard outside the convent, and the windows that had been sealed shut with the blessed screws blew open with no resistance. The sisters shut the windows again using more blessed screws. It is said that over the years, each time the windows were blown open, they were blessed and sealed again with new screws.

The legend states that vampires had traveled in these caskets under the protection of the girls, whose families had cared for the aristocratic vampires for centuries. The girls watched over the vampires and their caskets as they traveled together across the ocean and stayed with the caskets until they were stored at Ursuline on the third floor. On the first night after the arrival of the girls in New Orleans, the vampires slipped out of Ursuline to obtain more suitable living quarters in the city. The caskets remained at Ursuline as a place for the vampires to hide undetected when visiting the girls so that they could communicate with the girls in privacy. It was said that when they did visit the girls, they would enter through the third-story windows, and the blessed screws did little to stop them, as they would blow open the windows and enter at their will.

One has to wonder why vampires would choose to be delivered to a convent of all places when traveling to a strange land. It is here where the legend grows even more intriguing.

The Ursulines are reportedly named after Saint Ursula, who was the daughter of a fifth-century king in Europe. Ursula was to be married off to the son of a pagan king in accordance with her father's wishes. Desiring to remain a virgin, she planned a delay in the hopes of talking him out of the marriage by making a list of demands that would have to be met before she would agree to the marriage. She asked for 11,000 virgin girls to accompany her on a pilgrimage, where she would travel for three years and dedicate her life to God. She also asked that her pagan fiancé must agree to convert to Christianity.

To her surprise, her father, the pagan king, and his son agreed to her terms. During the three-year journey, Ursula received a message from an angel who told her that she was going to be martyred during her journey. According to the legend, as Ursula visited Cologne, Germany, she, along with the 11,000 virgin girls, was captured and killed by Attila the Hun's men, which is described as being martyred in the Catholic religion. Ursula was reportedly 11 years old at the time when she and the other young girls were killed.

Ursula has inspired many to honor her name, including Christopher Columbus, who named the Virgin Islands for her, and Magellan, who named Cape Virgenes for her. However, many scholars believe this Catholic legend to be a derivative of the pagan goddess Freya, a Germanic goddess who welcomes the souls of virgin girls into the afterlife and is associated with love, fertility, and the cycle of life of birth, death, and rebirth.

Under the protection of the goddess Freya/Saint Ursula, these young virgin girls traveled by ship just as Ursula did, knowing that they were being sent on a voyage from their homes in Europe to New Orleans to be placed in arranged marriages.

Freya and Ursula were recognized throughout Europe as being protectors of virgin girls and deceased maidens. *The legend in New Orleans says that the caskets delivered that night with this particular group of girls were filled with female vampires, who were the symbolic deceased maidens making their voyage to the New World.*

These female vampires entered the world of New Orleans and created a powerful new lineage of vampires in the city, which reportedly remains to this day. While many vampire legends in New Orleans focus on the male vampires in the city, it is said that this was done purposefully, as the women worked hard to conceal their identities. Many were able to blend into society as their beauty and charm opened doors to Creole society. They reportedly worked with Voodoo priestesses and witches in the city, and provided aid and assistance to them and continue to do so today.

 KALA'S TRAVEL TIPS

- **Our Lady of Prompt Succor** is the patron saint of New Orleans and the state of Louisiana. Schools around the state, including the school my mother attended in Louisiana, are named for her. If you would like to pray to Our Lady of Prompt Succor for quick aid, the best time to do so is on her feast day, which is January 8.

- In the garden around the convent there are **statues of patron saints of New Orleans and others, which are referred to as saints-in-waiting.** Catholic church doctrine requires three stages to sainthood, beginning with being listed as a venerable, which describes the heroism and virtues of the person being considered. The next stage is referred to as blessed, where one miraculous event is attributed to the person through his or her prayers or actions. In the third stage, the person is listed as a saint, where two or more miracles are reported in his or her name. Statues of saints in the Ursuline Gardens include St. Frances Xavier Cabrini, who became the first American saint; St. Katharine Drexel, who founded Xavier, the only African-American Catholic university in the United States; and St. Philippine Duchesne, who founded the Sacred Heart Society in America.

- The statue of Our Lady of Prompt Succor was later moved to the **National Shrine of Our Lady of Prompt Succor,** located on the State Street campus of Ursuline Academy. Prayers are made to her before every hurricane asking for help before the coming storm. Ursuline Academy is the oldest continuously operating school for girls in the United States.

- The **Old Ursuline Convent** is located at 1100 Chartres Street. Both the church and the convent are open for tours daily.

- The **blessed screws and windows** on the third floor have long since been replaced with hurricane-rated windows and shutters. The legends state the vampires no longer live near the convent, but that on occasion they return to walk the grounds.

- When Louisiana was purchased by the United States, seven of the Ursuline nuns decided to be proactive and defend their property. They wrote a **letter to President Thomas Jefferson,** requesting that the property rights be granted to the sisters of Ursuline Convent by the US government. The president agreed in an eloquent response by letter, which can be viewed inside the convent.

CHAPTER 9

Guests in Spirit Still Attend the Quadroon Balls at the Bourbon Orleans

"Mac Rebennack, better known as Dr. John, once told me that when a brass band plays at a small club back up in one of the neighborhoods, it's as if the audience—dancing, singing to the refrains, laughing—is part of the band. They are two parts of the same thing. The dancers interpret, or it might be better to say literally embody, the sounds of the band, answering the instruments. Since everyone is listening to different parts of the music—she to the trumpet melody, he to the bass drum, she to the trombone—the audience is a working model in three dimensions of the music, a synesthesic transformation of materials. And of course, the band is also watching the dancers, and getting ideas from the dancers' gestures. The relationship between band and audience is in that sense like the relationship between two lovers making love, where cause and effect becomes very hard to see, even impossible to call by its right name; one is literally getting down, as in particle physics, to some root stratum where one is freed from the lockstep of time itself, where time might even run backward, or sideways, and something eternal and transcendent is accessed."

—Tom Piazza, *Why New Orleans Matters*

THE TERM *QUADROON* was defined in the Old South as a person who was of mixed race, which included being one-quarter black descent. This description was typically defined as

The Bourbon Orleans Hotel, where the quadroon balls were once held

the child of a person of white ancestry and a person described as a mulatto, which is a person born from one white parent and one black parent.

Many quadroon women came from Haiti, and their beauty was described as being so elegant that they were referred to as *Les Sirenes*, after the tales of the mythological sirens who captivated the hearts of men with their stunning beauty. The law at this time said that quadroon women could not marry white men, even though many men professed their love for them. There were few choices available to these women, and so becoming a mistress was one of the best options at the time.

Their stunning beauty and sensuality caused quite a stir when they appeared publicly, so much so that some of the wealthy white women in New Orleans campaigned for the governor to issue an edict declaring that the quadroon women could not wear hats with plumes in public nor could they wear the jewelry given to them by wealthy men. The edict also stated that their hair could not be seen in public and that they must wear scarves, called tignons, to cover their heads.

There was great resentment between some of the white women and quadroon women, as the wives many times fought with their husbands, who took the side of their quadroon mistresses and often chose to spend more time with them than their wives. In many of these relationships, the quadroon mistress did indeed possess the lure of the siren call that the men could not ignore. Many of the men professed to love their mistresses more than their wives, often having been forced to marry the white woman to produce legal heirs for their fortunes and for social or political connections between families. The jealousy only grew in these wives, who often had to see their husband's mistress at the theater, where the wives were seated in one location while the quadroon mistresses were seated in a nearby section. It was also said that many of these men took the opportunity to slip their quadroon mistresses into the masked balls during Mardi Gras, where they could dance with them undetected behind the elaborate wigs, masks, gloves, and full ball gowns.

In New Orleans, wealthy Creole men often took a quadroon woman as a lover and companion, setting these women up with their own homes and providing for their welfare and for their children. The men continued these relationships throughout their lifetime, even as they went on to marry white women and set up families in this capacity as well. It was well known throughout Creole society that these men had children with their quadroon mistresses, and these children were lovingly cared for and provided for. The children were often sent to France to be educated, as it was illegal at the time for anyone who was not white to be educated in the United States. These children would return after their education in France as free people of color and established themselves in the city with the assistance of their fathers.

The spiritual presence of the Catholic nuns is felt in the city.

Due to social standards and European customs, a meeting place was required where the wealthy men could be introduced to eligible quadroon women to converse with them and decide whom they would like to partner with long term. To fulfill this need, quadroon balls were arranged, where the men could dance and socialize with the young women. The parents of these women also attended these balls, and arrangements were typically made between the young woman's parents and the interested man. Financial compensation was given to the parents, and contractual agreements were put into place, which included furnishing a home for the young woman, claiming ownership of any children born from the union, and providing a guarantee that the young woman and her offspring would be cared for with all the material needs to live properly.

These balls were considered social events in New Orleans. Among the Creole men it was a mark of social distinction, class, and privilege to have a quadroon mistress, which showcased both the wealth of the man as well as proof of his virility and vigor. The men eagerly awaited the announcement of the quadroon balls each year. The social season typically began in October and ran through the season of Mardi Gras into the next year. No expense was spared at these balls, with lavish displays of food, live music, and brilliant decor displayed at each one.

The women were dressed in elaborate gowns during the events and were presented in a fashion similar to a debutante ball. As the partnerships were arranged, the women moved swiftly into their new home and role as a mistress. For many of these women, they also went on to become entrepreneurs, establishing businesses of their own as hairdressers, dressmakers, and nurses. Some of them also built their craft on Voodoo and sold their wares, including love potions, gris-gris bags, and other amulets and talismans.

At one point during the height of New Orleans wealth before the Civil War, more than 30 locations were reported to hold quadroon balls throughout the city, which is a testament to the popularity of this practice.

Perhaps the most well-known historical location for these balls is the building now known as the Bourbon Orleans Hotel. Built in 1817, the original building was created as an opulent and acclaimed ballroom, known as the Orleans Ballroom, which offered fine dining and dancing. It also had the attached Orleans Theater next door, offering the best in French opera entertainment. The balls held at this location had a reputation for being some of the most elaborate and stunning, so much so that it appeared that some of these attendees never wanted the evenings to end. The stories of ghost sightings at this location say that some of the women who attended the quadroon balls have lingered on in the afterlife, still dancing and sashaying in their evening gowns, hoping for one last dance with a hand-some gentleman.

Guests at the hotel throughout the years have reported see-ing one particular young woman from this era. She is described as irresistibly beautiful with almond-shaped eyes and dark upswept hair, with a jeweled comb tucked behind her ear. The rustling sound of her ball gown is often heard before she appears. Witnesses report hearing music playing and see her dancing and humming to the music. She appears to be stuck in this moment, all dressed up and preparing for her big eve-ning of dancing. She never appears to notice the guests who see her, nor does she interact with anyone in the hotel. She simply appears looking stunning, and as the music plays, she dances and sways in her beautiful gown, only to disappear again a few moments later. Other guests have reported seeing her in the evenings on the balcony of the hotel, wrapping her arms around a young man in an intimate and loving fashion.

As the Civil War changed the destiny of New Orleans, the building was sold to the Sisters of the Holy Family, the oldest female-led African-American Catholic nun order in the United States. The four women who established the order turned the building into a convent and school, and the Orleans Ballroom was used as their chapel. Later in the 1960s, the building was placed back up for sale, and it was purchased and renovated into the Bourbon Orleans Hotel.

Due to the history and legacy of the property, the hotel is considered to be one of the most haunted hotels in the city, with more than 20 different types of ghosts and hundreds of paranormal activities reported in the hotel on a regular basis. There are an impressive number of reports by guests and staff, who have seen the ghost of the Confederate soldier who walks the halls at night on the sixth and seventh floor of the property, pacing up and down as if expecting trouble to arrive at any

Horse head posts are found throughout the French Quarter of New Orleans, where horses and horse-drawn carriages would use the rings to tie up the horses on the street.

moment. He carries a gun and quietly walks back and forth as if on guard duty, and occasionally tobacco smoke can be smelled before he appears.

Ghost children are frequently reported playing throughout the hotel, and ghosts of young women are often seen, both of which are attributed to the times when the nuns owned the property and, along with a school, provided a medical facility and orphanage. It appears that some of the children who were cared for during this time died while under medical care, and their spirits remain on the property, playing in the halls. They often are heard laughing, shouting, and running down the halls so loudly at times that guests will open the doors to see why children are running around so late at night, only to see the ghost children and watch them disappear before their eyes or to see nothing at all. Many locals surmise that the children most likely perished during the yellow fever epidemics in New Orleans. Due to the feverish state they were in when they died, the children may not have realized that they were dead and, instead, woke up feeling better and went back to playing in the orphanage as they did each day.

Most of the ghosts appear to go about their daily and evening business, dancing, patrolling the halls, and playing, yet there is one guest who is frequently seen in the lobby who does not care for visitors. Described as an elderly gentleman, he appears to enjoy spending late afternoons seated in the lobby area while reading the daily paper and smoking a cigar. His ghostly apparition is so solid that many people reportedly mistake him as a guest and ask him to extinguish his cigar as the smoke is bothering them. When this interaction occurs, he is reported to give them a haughty look, stand up angrily, gather his paper, and march away, when he then disappears into thin air. It's easy to imagine the shocked look of the guest who, having just insulted the man, now discovers they were talking to a ghost. I would think that if they ran into him again during their stay, the encounter would not be as pleasant, which is a good reminder to be kind and polite to strangers you meet everywhere.

One of my favorite reports about the ghosts at the hotel came from several locals I met in a bar on Bourbon Street, who shared with me what they had heard about the haunted Bourbon Orleans Hotel. They said there once was a guest who stumbled back to the hotel after an evening of heavy drinking on Bourbon Street. He was very loud and rude and had become disorderly in the halls, speaking profanity and being a drunken public nuisance in general. As he was walking down the halls in this manner, he experienced the feeling of being slapped hard on his hand. Stunned, he looked up to see a nun standing in front of him. His friends reported hearing the slap and seeing a red mark on his hand after the incident. Growing up in Catholic school myself, I remember the slaps from the nuns, and this would not be surprising at all to hear that they are still patrolling the halls in the afterlife. They definitely would not like to hear profanity or to see someone wandering the halls late at night while being loud and rude. It's nice to know that good manners are still being impressed upon visitors and locals alike in the good establishment.

 KALA'S TRAVEL TIPS

- The best place reported to see the **dancing quadroon girl** is under the chandelier in the ballroom in the late evening.
- Check out **Napoleon's Itch** for music and cocktails, and try the **Voodoo Mojo Cocktail** at the Bourbon Oh!
- The **Bourbon Orleans Hotel** is a great location to stay in the heart of all of the festivities. Just remember to be quiet in the hallways when returning back to the hotel in the late evening, so you won't upset the ghost nuns patrolling the hallways.
- Paranormal researchers report great results at this hotel with photographs, video, and EVP recordings. **Don't forget your camera** and other equipment on this trip.

CHAPTER 10

Ghostly Carriage Rides at the Old French Opera House on Bourbon Street

"At one point, early on, some public figures even asked whether it 'made sense' to rebuild New Orleans. Would you let your own mother die because it didn't make financial sense to spend the money to treat her, or because you were too busy to spend the time to heal her sick spirit?"

—Tom Piazza, *Why New Orleans Matters*

THE FRENCH OPERA first arrived in New Orleans in 1776, with performances offered in small venues around the city to the delight of the Creole society. As the city grew and the demand for artistic performances increased, the decision was made to build an opera venue in the French Quarter. In 1859, at the astronomical cost for that time of $118,000, the French Opera House was built in the French Quarter on the corners of Bourbon Street and Toulouse; it quickly became a treasured landmark. Architecturally designed by James Gallier, the building was considered to be a masterpiece of Greek architecture and featured an elliptical auditorium where 1,800 people sat in four tiers of seating. As was customary for the times, special screened boxes were installed so that ladies in mourning, pregnant women, mistresses, and madams could discreetly attend the performances.

In Creole society, attending the French Opera House was the height of the social entertainment season. It provided an opportunity to enjoy the performance and to be seen by one's peers. For

Bourbon Street side view of the Inn on Bourbon, site of the Old French Opera House, where carriages once pulled up filled with patrons

more than 60 years, until 1919 when it burned to the ground, the Opera House was one of the most distinctive and cherished locations in the French Quarter. While opera was the main attraction and focus of the house, it also hosted balls during Carnival as well as a variety of charity benefits, receptions, and other events.

The Opera House soon established itself as the social icon for New Orleans. During the height of its reign, the social season (as it was described by the elite high society in New Orleans) began each year with the first performance held at the Opera House. Each year, everyone looked forward with anticipation to this grand beginning to the season, where they would socialize with other families, introduce young debutantes to society, mix and mingle for business and pleasure, and show off their latest fashions, jewelry, and other displays of wealth.

At this historic location, the only physical mark left standing where the French Opera House stood is an indention in

THE FRENCH OPERA HOUSE

The INN ON BOURBON, on the corner of Toulouse and Bourbon Streets, rests on the site of the Old French Opera House, for 60 years, the cultural center of New Orleans Creole society, and the first opera house in the United States. Erected in 1859 at a cost of $118,000.00, it was opened to the public on December 1, 1859. The opera house was one of the most famous masterpieces designed by noted architect James Gallier, architect of Gallier Hall and many other classic 18th Century buildings.

A plaque commemorating the French Opera House

the brick cobblestones along the street where horse-drawn carriages once pulled at the front entrance to drop off the elegantly dressed Creoles. Photographs of the French Opera House show that the building displayed a curved appearance at the corner of Bourbon and Toulouse. The building now standing at this location is the Inn on Bourbon. The inn followed a similar architectural design, including the nod to Greek architecture once featured at the Opera House.

As a young girl growing up in Louisiana, I remember the first time my parents took me to the Mardi Gras parades in New Orleans. During the day we walked through the quarter, and I was drawn to this particular location each time we passed by, as it felt very familiar to me. Later that night, as we slept at a hotel further down the quarter, I dreamed about this location, and in my dream, the location changed to look like the old French Opera House, which years later I was able to confirm in photographs.

Toulouse Street side view of the Inn on Bourbon, where the old ghost with white hair is said to walk down the street

In my dream, I was attending an event at the French Opera House. I remember the feeling of excitement about my new dress and loving the sound it made as I swished about when I moved. I also remember having to concentrate on walking properly as a young lady. At the Opera House, I recognized other people at the event, some whom I liked and others whom I knew were not my friends.

The next morning, I told my mother about my dream in the best way I could describe it as a child. She listened politely while putting on her makeup and preparing for us to go out again that day. No more was discussed about the dream at that time, and I soon put it out of my thoughts, as I've always had at least three vivid dreams each night that I remember the next day.

Years later as an adult, I was planning a trip to New Orleans with my husband and randomly selected a hotel for us to stay, which was the Inn on Bourbon. My main intent was to find a great location for us to be close to everything we wanted to do in the French Quarter. Upon our arrival to the inn, I was delighted with the hotel and found the architecture charming and the location superb. Excited to get out and see the quarter, we dropped our bags in our room and headed out to have dinner and enjoy the evening. As soon as you arrive in New Orleans, you feel the urge to have a good meal, which announces to the city that you are back. This is an old custom, and it is considered that you are never truly back in the city until you have your first good meal. Not one to ignore ancient customs and rituals, my husband and I were quickly off in search of that first great meal, which is easy to find in the French Quarter.

Later that evening, we returned back to the Inn on Bourbon and climbed into bed ready to sleep. As soon as my head hit the pillow, I began to dream about the French Opera House. The dream was eerily similar to the one I had as a little girl where I saw the event in great detail.

By the time I woke the next morning, I had experienced a series of dreams all relating back to the time when the Opera House was in existence in New Orleans. I realized that this was the inn that I had walked by as a little girl with my parents. Each night as I slept in the inn, I continued to have these dreams and to remember the events that I had attended in a previous lifetime as a young woman in New Orleans. Each morning as I awoke, I would share these dreams with my husband, describing to him the vivid details that occurred here at this location in the past. It was a wonderful feeling of coming home and feeling attached to a place in the most beautiful manner, removing the concept of time and previous lifetimes and blending them into one.

The last night that we stayed in the hotel, we had made arrangements to have dinner at Arnaud's. It was early in the evening, and I stepped outside the hotel to enjoy the cool evening air while waiting for my husband. He was inside accessing the ATM to get cash to indulge my habit of tipping street performers on every corner, ducking in various shops for tarot readings, and buying trinkets in stores as we walked along the streets each evening.

I noticed that it was a bit quiet on Bourbon Street, as the steady stream of crowds and noise had not yet hit their full roar for the evening. While waiting in front of the hotel, I began to walk along the sidewalk where the famous indention is seen along the cobblestones, where the horse-drawn carriages once pulled up to drop off passengers at the Opera House entrance.

I turned away from the street for a moment to see if my husband was coming through the door, but he was not yet in sight. As I did, the sound of horse hooves clopping on the street caught my attention, and I turned back around, expecting to see one of the tour guides coming down Bourbon Street with the mule-drawn carriages they use for tours. As I turned, to my surprise, I did see a horse-drawn carriage arriving at the Inn on Bourbon, but the image itself was not from the present day. It was a ghost carriage, complete with a ghost driver. As I continued to stare, the doors opened and a ghost man and woman exited the carriage and stood before me, as they straightened their clothing before preparing to enter the building. I turned to look at the inn, now expecting it to look like a ghostly version of the French Opera House, but it had not changed in appearance.

The couple took no notice of me or anyone else walking by on Bourbon Street. They simply composed themselves and then walked through a wall of the Inn on Bourbon building and disappeared. Once they were gone from my sight, I turned back to see if the carriage was still there, but the carriage and driver had also disappeared into thin air.

The next time I visited New Orleans in late November, I stayed at the inn again, and these events repeated themselves in almost the same manner, including the series of dreams regarding my past life and again seeing the carriage arrive with the ghost man and woman at the front entrance one very cold evening. When inquiring with locals about the history of the French Opera House, several shared ghost stories with me that they had been told by the street artists who perform here many nights throughout the year. They said that these performers report experiencing a strong whooshing feeling, as if a carriage had quickly rushed by them, when nothing was actually physically there. They also shared that on some occasions when they experienced this phenomenon, the local policemen who patrol this area on horseback in the evenings would notice that their horses had become agitated and uncomfortable at the same time. Many of the performers wondered if the horses could sense the ghost driver and horses as they pulled up to deliver their passengers to another performance at the French Opera House.

Each time that I visit and stay at the Inn on Bourbon, my dreams are longer and more vivid in detail. I hope in time to put all the pieces together from this experience, which would be fascinating.

KALA'S TRAVEL TIPS

- There are other ghost stories reported around this location. The balconies from the rooms on the Toulouse street side of the hotel are known for being good places to view the **ghost witch named Marguerite,** who reportedly walks down Toulouse Street some evenings on her way to visit the old cottage where she lived near Royal Street. Those who have seen her report hearing the sound of wailing and see a white mist first appear before seeing the old woman with long white hair. The legend states that she was a Storyville madam who had been betrayed by her lover, and she sought revenge against him and the new woman he was dating. Viewing this ghost woman from a balcony might be the safest place to see her. Those who report bumping into her on the street report the experience to be very frightening, as she portrays a haglike appearance and acts like a banshee.

- **The Inn on Bourbon has some of the best balconies** on Bourbon Street connected to the front rooms, which provide an incredible front-row seat to all of the activities on Bourbon Street day and night. You'll also be greeted with all of the sights and sounds of Bourbon Street until the wee hours of the morning, so if you are looking for a quiet night's sleep, it's best to ask for one of the quieter rooms with a courtyard view instead.

- The inn is conveniently located and within **walking distance** of almost every place you'd like to visit in the French Quarter, making it a great place as your home base while visiting New Orleans. You're only steps away from some of the best bars, music, food, entertainment, and shopping, including Pat O'Brien's a block away and a four-block walk to Jackson Square.

- The **Puccini Bar** inside the Inn on Bourbon offers free opera performances on some nights in the bar, bringing back the romance of this special history.

- The best time to experience the **ghost carriage driver and passengers** is in the fall and winter seasons, as they seem to appear during the time that would be customary for the social season. For paranormal researchers, the difficulty would be to get any distinctive EVP recordings or video, as the streets are filled with music, noise, people, and blinking neon lights when the ghosts arrive in the evening by carriage. Like many ghostly experiences, the highlight of the experience is to experience it as it occurs. The ghostly passengers and driver do not appear to be aware that time and the location has changed around them, and they show no interest or awareness of others or in communicating with anyone directly. Their focus appears to be entering the Opera House to attend the event that evening.

CHAPTER 11

The Monk Who Saved the Children at the Place d'Armes Hotel

"About fifteen miles above New Orleans the river goes very slowly. It has broadened out there until it is almost a sea and the water is yellow with the mud of half a continent. Where the sun strikes it, it is golden."

—Frank Yerby, *The Foxes of Harrow*

LOCATED ON ST. ANN STREET in the French Quarter, the Place d'Armes hotel is located just a few steps away from St. Louis Cathedral and Jackson Square. With around 84 rooms based on brick town houses, the hotel is often described as charming, intimate, and lovingly restored with historic details. It also has a lush courtyard filled with magnolia trees, crepe myrtles, and bougainvillea, complemented by fountains and statues, making this spot one of the most photographed courtyards in the French Quarter. This hotel also has the reputation of being one of the haunted hotels in New Orleans.

Before the hotel stood in this location, it was the site of the first school in Louisiana, established in 1725. A sign is inscribed on the property, which shares the history of the school and reads: "Site of the First Louisiana School, 1725. On this site, Father Raphael de Luxembourg Capuchin, Pastor of the Parish Church of St. Louis (later the Cathedral), opened the first school in French Colonial Louisiana."

The original house, which served as the school, was purchased from Augustin Langlois. The Ursuline nuns arrived

Entrance to the Place d'Armes Hotel

two years later in 1727 to establish the girls' school at the Ursuline Convent.

While the first Louisiana school was in operation, the Great Fire of New Orleans erupted on the blustery day of March 21, 1788. What began as a small fire in a home near Jackson Square, where a candle caught a curtain ablaze, soon spread throughout the city, as no alarm was sounded. This allowed the fire to rage quickly out of control. Fueled by a strong wind, the fire destroyed nearly 900 out of a total of 1,100 buildings in the French Quarter. The destruction totaled almost 90% of the city, including the Cabildo and the hospital. What had taken the residents of New Orleans decades to build as a city now lay before them, destroyed in only a matter of hours.

The Great Fire occurred on Good Friday. Due to the religious protocols and observation of this day, the priests and

A sign depicting the early days of New Orleans, when Jackson Square was called Plaza D'Armas

monks were forbidden to ring the church bells for any reason. Ringing the church bells was the established method in the city to warn residents of danger, and the bells would have quickly alerted residents to the fire. This warning would have given people more time to escape from the devastation and rally others to gather and fight the fire. The legend states that the priests stood nearby, refusing to ring the bells, and instead prayed for divine intervention while the city burned around them.

The first Louisiana school was located close to where the fire first began, and reportedly some of the boys and men in the school were trapped inside the building during the fire. The school was located just steps away from Jackson Square, and everyone was caught off guard with how quickly the fire spread, leaving them all with little time to evacuate.

In addition, there were only two fire carriages in the city of New Orleans. Due to the late warning of danger, residents were facing insurmountable odds. Both of the carriages were quickly destroyed, as the fire raged through multiple streets, claiming everything in its path.

The legend states that during the chaos, one brave monk risked his life in the fire. He ran back into the first Louisiana school over and over, braving the fire and smoke to pull as many boys as he could to safety. During these heroic efforts, the legend states that he died a day or two later, perhaps from the overexertion, smoke inhalation, or (as some say) a heart attack. Reportedly his spirit still remains here on the property. Each year on March 21, witnesses claim that he appears in the midafternoon and can be seen rushing in and out of the building as he leads the boys to safety outside. Some people claim to hear shouting and calls for help. The ghostly reenactment is said to last only a minute or so before the monk vanishes almost as quickly as he appeared.

Before the school was built on this location, a house had stood here on St. Ann. Some of the most popular ghost stories appear to be connected to the occupants of this former home. Guests report seeing a grandmotherly looking ghost who roams the halls, enters their rooms, and shushes them if they are too loud and rowdy at night. When they see her or awaken to see her standing near their bed, she soon disappears in front of their eyes.

The grandmother ghost is believed to be one of the occupants from the original home when it was here in New Orleans. The grandmother ghost stays on the property, and, while harmless, she prefers that guests keep a respectful tone of voice, especially in the evening. Little else is known about the home that originally stood here, with the exception that it was purchased from Augustin Langlois, but the grandmother appears to have remained behind, centuries after the home has gone.

A wide variety of eerie paranormal occurrences are reported by both staff and guests at the Place d'Armes hotel, including phone calls to the front desk in the middle of the night from rooms that are empty and the sounds of ghost children playing in the courtyard area. There's also a report from a guest traveling with her children who woke up in the middle of the night to find the children's toys pulled out after they were picked up for the evening. The toys were scattered around the room as if they were played with during the night. The guest also reported that the children described having fun playing with their new friends in the courtyard. When the parents asked to meet the new friends, the children pointed to an area where they claimed to see the children, but the adults were unable to see anyone there.

The grandmotherly ghost seems to enjoy looking after the ghost children residing there, and by most reports, they seem to cohabitate nicely. While seeing a ghost might be unsettling to some people, the actual incidents reported here at the hotel are of a positive and heartwarming nature with no ill intention toward anyone staying at the hotel. The only time any sadness is reported around these paranormal events is during the appearance of the monk on March 21, and even during this paranormal event the sadness is based on his urgency to save the boys from the fire. His bravery and dedication are a testimony to his love for the children, and he returns each year in a brave attempt to finish the job at hand.

While the monk can be linked historically with the fire at the school, and the grandmother can be placed during the time that the building was a personal residence, the ghost who is not yet identified is an elderly gentleman dressed in 1800s garb. Witnesses say that he is always polite, tipping his hat and nodding when encountering guests in the lobby. Perhaps he visits the hotel in the hopes of meeting up with the grandmother ghost and spending some time in her company.

KALA'S TRAVEL TIPS

- Place d'Armes is one of the hotels closest to **Café du Monde,** home of the best beignets in the world. Slip out early every morning to enjoy a few beignets and coffee, and then head back to your bed to enjoy a few more winks of sleep.

- The hotel is also close to the **French Market,** which is great for shopping. Bring a tote bag with you to haul your treasures back to the hotel.

- Barring the anniversary of the fire on March 21, the **ghosts** seen every other day of the year are warm and welcoming and truly seem to enjoy mingling with the guests. If you've always wanted to see a ghost or have a ghostly experience, this is a friendly way to have your first experience. According to many reports, ghostly noises include the sound of children play-ing in the hall, the elevator opening at random with no one inside, and full apparitions in the hallway, including the ghost of a little girl dressed in a nightgown who knocks on the door. When the guest opens the door, she asks if her grandmother is inside. Before the surprised guest can answer, she fades away in front of them.

CHAPTER 12

A Loving Legacy at the Cornstalk Hotel

"There is something haunting in the light of the moon; it has all the dispassionateness of a disembodied soul, and something of its inconceivable mystery."

—Joseph Conrad, *Lord Jim*

HAVE YOU EVER VISITED LOUISIANA? The climate of the Deep South is quite different than other parts of the country. The humidity smacks you in the face the moment you step off the plane. The air feels heavy, moist, and damp, with temperatures running hotter than the gumbo. Spanish moss drips from the trees, and the land is lush and green, with a hint of danger lurking in these ancient gardens as water moccasins and rattlesnakes slither through the grass and often hang from trees, to the surprise of boaters nearby. Alligators float by undetected in the bayou, looking like a log in the water until you notice their eyes right above the water line, following your every move. Hopefully that is all you see, rather than the rush of enormous jaws snapping at you from the levee.

The storms here are legendary and phenomenal. As a little girl, I could sense a storm brewing while it was still miles away. It first began with the tiniest shift in the breeze, and then the wind would rustle through the trees as if to whisper that danger was on its way. The trees began to sway, their branches reaching out to each other as if to carry the message from limb to limb across the fields. The skies would soon darken and the humidity would build to such an unbearably high degree that even the drone of insects and frogs would hush, as everyone held their breath for a moment, finding the air almost impossible to breathe. Just when it feels that you cannot bear the oppressive buildup of heat and humidity a moment longer, the wind rushes through, quickly followed by the first splatters of rain and the loud crackling of thunder announcing the oncoming lightning storm.

Every living thing with any common sense soon runs for cover. Once the storm has passed, creatures large and small venture back out onto the land. The mosquitoes begin their flight in full force, accompanied by the drone of crickets and hundreds of other insects and bugs. The swampy areas of Louisiana overflow with this natural life, and in the early days of New Orleans, one had to venture only a few miles outside the city into South Louisiana to be greeted by the bayous and swampy areas.

I grew up surrounded by these swamps, levees, and storms, and I loved them. I've also seen the shock and awe of others who are not from the Deep South when they first experience this type of climate that is completely foreign to them. Imagine then, if more than 150 years ago, you married the man you loved, and he moved you far away from the only home you had ever known and brought you to New Orleans. You'd have no idea what to expect because you're from Iowa, and for your entire life, the land that you are familiar with has fields of grain and corn and fresh lakes. Swamps and alligators are something you've never heard of, much less seen before. As you begin your new life in New Orleans, everything is unfamiliar to you—the weather, the culture, the gardens, the customs, even the language, and the food. No matter how great the love is that you share with your husband, a tiny part of you longs for the home and family you left behind, and you wish only to have a link to comfortable and familiar surroundings.

The historic Cornstalk Hotel

This is where our tale of the haunted Cornstalk Hotel begins, with the story of a husband's love for his bride—a love so dear and strong that he wanted to comfort and surround her with a familiar scene from Iowa in the only manner he could in the sinking wetlands of Louisiana.

The Cornstalk Hotel was originally built as a home in 1816 for Judge Francois Xavier-Martin, who is best known in Louisiana as a former chief justice for the Supreme Court. The home was designed according to his wishes, but the records show that several homes had previously been built on this property, beginning in 1730. Each of the previous homes had been destroyed by fire, most likely by the two Great Fires of New Orleans—the first that destroyed 90% of the French Quarter and the second that destroyed more than 200 buildings. The records of who owned the homes before Judge Martin are missing (some were destroyed by fire), but it is assumed by most historians that several families lived at this location over the decades.

In 1834 Dr. Joseph Secondo Biamenti purchased the home for himself and his Iowa bride. He ordered a cast-iron fence to be installed around the property. In New Orleans, lovely homes with cast-iron balconies and fences are features found in great abundance on every corner of the city, so these materials on their own are not what has made the Cornstalk Hotel famous.

What causes this building to stand out in the French Quarter is that the cast-iron fence resembles cornstalks, as if one was looking out at a field of corn made completely from cast iron. Each column of the fence is anchored with a pumpkin. Then climbing up each iron post are vines, leaves, and flowers, until you reach the top of the post, where cornstalks are partially open to display the kernels of corn inside.

The effect is whimsical, and the artisan must have worked long hours to shape iron into such delicate and intricate pieces, which include a butterfly landing on the front gate. The good doctor loved his wife dearly. Knowing that the swampy soil in New Orleans would never allow a field of corn to grow, he did the next best thing he could to bring an Iowa cornfield to his wife by designing the iron fence cornstalks, so that whenever she looked out the window she would be reminded of her home.

Architecturally, the hotel is fascinating. It is listed in a multitude of travel guidebooks as a must-see location to photograph in the city. Yet this hotel meets that list for other reasons, including the legends of ghosts haunting the hotel. Guests have reported hearing children laughing as their footsteps pitter-patter back and forth inside the house and outside.

The nearby Andrew Jackson Hotel was originally a boys' boarding school, and one of the yellow fever epidemics in New Orleans spread quickly through the school. Some of the boys died during this epidemic, and the popular theory is that the ghost children seen at the Cornstalk Hotel are these schoolboys who enjoy playing in both buildings.

Cast-iron gates lead to the beautiful entrance of the Cornstalk Hotel.

There are also reports of hotel guests hearing the sounds of someone tapping on the window, only to find no one there when they pull back the curtain. They also report doors opening and closing in the middle of the night.

At the hotel, I was psychically drawn to spend time outdoors rather than inside the building. The iron fence is quite captivating, and there is something almost electric about it. Iron was used in cemeteries, as it has a reputation of keeping spirits inside the area surrounded by iron or preventing them from entering an area surrounded by an iron fence, as ancient tales state that spirits are not able to cross over iron fences and gates.

This particular iron fence vibrated with an energy that I had not noticed elsewhere in the French Quarter. The fence emanated a blue hue, as if it was magnetized with an energy field. It had the look and feel of a spell, as if someone who knew what they were doing had magically placed a charm on the fence for purposes yet unknown.

As I tuned into the fence to determine what energy had been placed there, I followed the blue auric field and saw that it surrounded the property. Protective spells had been placed in this field to protect the hotel from any harm.

The hotel certainly has a warm and welcoming feel about it. If you are standing in front of the fence from the street and want to see this blue energy field for yourself, you'll find that the left side of the fence has the most energy, as if it wants to protect itself from energy coming from that direction. On the right side, the energy field is much more open and relaxed, appearing to not detect any harm coming from this side. This right side of the property is where the ghost boys are most often seen playing on the lawn.

As I continued to study the fence and the supernatural energy attached to it, I had the distinct feeling of being watched. I looked up at the hotel and saw a woman looking out at me from an upstairs window. I gave a friendly wave to her, thinking she was a guest, until I noticed that she was wearing a dark dress with a lace collar at the neck and had her hair pulled back into a tight bun.

My first thought was that she was dressed in period clothing, perhaps for an event at the hotel. This thought soon vanished, however, for as I stood there looking at her, she disappeared into thin air except for one of her hands, which remained there at the window for a few moments longer. She appeared to me as someone who was very protective and inquisitive about the comings and goings at the hotel.

My encounter with the woman was very brief. She was quite a distance away, as I was outside near the fence looking up and she was upstairs inside the hotel, so there wasn't a strong connection. The one thing I did feel strongly, however, was that she was not the wife of Dr. Biamenti. This woman appeared to be dressed more in the style of the late 1700s rather than the mid-1800s, when Dr. Biamenti and his wife lived in the home. Most likely she was a previous occupant of the home that burned down during one of the fires in New Orleans.

 KALA'S TRAVEL TIPS

- The legend states that **Harriet Beecher Stowe** visited here while in New Orleans. It is unclear how she knew the owners or what the reason was for her visit to the Biamenti home. She had just come from seeing the slave markets in the city, which she later said inspired her to write *Uncle Tom's Cabin.*

- Located on **Royal Street,** the Cornstalk Hotel is in a great location in the French Quarter. More than 13 blocks of Royal Street are decorated with some of the most beautiful and ornate stretches of ironwork balconies and railings.

- Royal Street also has some of the best **shopping** in the French Quarter. Take your time and explore each shop, including art galleries, antique shops, and jewelry stores, to find unique treasures waiting inside.

- Two of my favorite restaurants are also on Royal Street, **Brennan's** and the **Court of Two Sisters.**

- A variety of **celebrities,** including Elvis Presley, have stayed at the Cornstalk Hotel.

CHAPTER 13

The Deathly Portal of Thirteen at Canal Street and City Park

"They told me to take a street-car named Desire, and then transfer to one called Cemeteries and ride six blocks and get off at—Elysian Fields!"

—Tennessee Williams, *A Streetcar Named Desire*

SOMETIMES, IN THE MOST MUNDANE of places, one finds sacred portals that reflect and connect with the circle of life and death. In New Orleans, there seem to be more than the average number of these types of portals found throughout the city. In fact, it's more difficult to find an area in the city not touched by spirituality and magic in some manner. One such magical area can be found at the crossroads of Canal Street and City Park Avenue, where the roads open up to the cities of the dead.

In 1964, the Canal Street Streetcar Line was disbanded when city planners decided that it was time to modernize New Orleans and remove the outdated transportation methods. This was later determined to have been a serious error in judgment for the city, as it succeeded only in removing the unique charm and flavor that energizes New Orleans and charms tourists. Forty years later in 2004, the Canal Street Streetcar Line was reinstated to the delight of residents and tourists alike and was touted as a local treasure and historic testament to the unique qualities of the city. The streetcars on this route were marked once again with the title Cemeteries, as Tennessee Williams so vividly described.

Cemeteries in New Orleans resemble small cities.

Thousands of residents and visitors travel back and forth on this line each day to work, to sightsee, and to visit various restaurants and shops. The 5.5-mile route begins at the French Market and continues along Canal Street through the Central Business District of the city. At the end of the 5-mile run, the streetcar line ends at City Park Avenue, where the cemeteries begin.

I've always found this particular streetcar line to be distinctly magical. One travels on the car through the bustle of city life only to arrive at the end of the line in front of the cemeteries. The streetcar serves as a carrier from the earthly world, eventually delivering the traveler to the underworld at the end of the line. This reminds me of the stories of the River Styx with the boat ferrying passengers from life to death.

The local legend and lore claims that there are 13 distinct cemeteries here at this crossroads, which spiritually intersect at this junction, making it a powerful portal and access point to the underworld.

The cemeteries reported to connect in one form or another here at this junction are Metairie; Cypress Grove; Odd Fellows Rest; St. Patrick #1, #2, and #3; Charity Hospital; St. John/Hope Mausoleum; Dispersed of Judah/Chevrah Thilim; Gates of Prayer; Masonic; Holt; and Greenwood.

Each cemetery, also referred to as a city of the dead in New Orleans, has its own haunted history within its gates. Following are just a few of the paranormal reports from each of them.

1. Metairie Cemetery

Established in 1872, Metairie Cemetery is one of the largest cemeteries in the area built on more than 150 acres. The site was formerly a horse-racing track, and the cemetery was designed in concentric oval rings alluding to its former history. By the time Metairie was organized as a cemetery, formal designs for cemeteries in the United States had grown in popularity. Metairie followed suit, making this cemetery more spacious in comparison to the older cemeteries in the city, where tombs are located very close to each other. Metairie is known for having some of the most ornate tombs in New Orleans. Elaborate designs throughout the grounds pay homage to Italian temples, the pyramids of Egypt, Celtic crosses, and Gothic architecture complete with gorgeous statues. A large number of Louisiana governors and mayors of New Orleans are buried in the cemetery, as well as other famous figures, including Jefferson Davis (president of the Confederate States of America) and more than 50 former kings and queens of Mardi Gras.

The cemetery is also the final resting place of many Confederate soldiers. Visitors report that not all of these soldiers are at rest, as many of their ghosts are seen walking the grounds at night in their uniforms.

The most famous haunting of all at Metairie is at the tomb of Josie Arlington, the famous madam from Storyville. Josie was

Elaborate vaults and tombs are built in the cities of the dead.

one of the most successful prostitutes in the city, and she built an impressive tomb to be buried in; it was made from red granite and included a statue of a young woman attempting to enter the door of the tomb. There have been a variety of explanations for this elaborate design. Some say that it was Josie wanting to find entry into the childhood home she had never had, as she was orphaned at the age of 4. Others say that it is representation of her code of conduct regarding the house of prostitution she ran, where no woman ever lost her virginity at her brothel. Others feel that it is simply a beautiful design that she saw somewhere and decided to copy the idea.

Regardless of which answer is the true reason for the design of her temple, the real intrigue begins after her death, when people began to report that her tomb was haunted. They reported that each night, a red light lit up the door of the tomb, similar to the lights once seen in the red-light district of the former whore-house area of Storyville. Witnesses also claimed seeing the ghost of Josie standing in front of the tomb in the evening, while others reported seeing the statue of the young girl become animated at night as it walked around the temple. These reports became so popular that huge crowds began to appear each evening looking for Josie's ghost and to see the red lights and moving statue.

Investigations regarding these allegations reported that a nearby traffic light was shining the red light onto the tomb, but others argued that if that were the case, why didn't a light shine on the tomb when the traffic light turned yellow or green?

Others stated that the red light stayed on the tomb well after the traffic light had changed and that the light was also seen floating around the statue and the tomb for long periods of time in the evening.

During this time, Josie's heirs had spent all of the money from Josie's trust and were no longer able to pay the upkeep of her tomb. This resulted in her burial site being foreclosed on, so Josie was moved to a nearby vault set aside for these types of situations while her trust went into bankruptcy. Her new internment site is undisclosed, which reportedly was done to help the crowds lose interest in visiting the tomb at night to look for her ghost.

This did little to stop the reports of hauntings around Josie's tomb, including hundreds of reports from people who still claim to have seen the statue become animated and walk around the tomb. Some say the animated statue lifts the bronze knocker on the tomb door and knocks on the door to gain entrance. This tomb is still one of the most popular to visit in Metairie Cemetery, though there are a considerable number of ornate mausoleums and monuments to visit throughout the site. Hundreds of ghostly sightings and reports roll in each year from a variety of locations in the cemetery, including sights of Civil War soldiers who still stand guard around the perimeter.

2. CYPRESS GROVE

Established in 1840 by the Fireman's Charitable and Benevolent Association, Cypress Grove is the resting place for the firemen who risked their lives fighting fires in the city, as well as for those who spent a life in service. The cemetery features the Irad Ferry monument, dedicated to the first member of the Fireman's Charitable and Benevolent Association killed in the line of duty in 1837. This monument has a broken column on top of the sarcophagus, which symbolizes a life cut short in its prime.

The two Great Fires of New Orleans in 1788 and 1794 together destroyed most of the French architecture in the city. It was rebuilt in a Spanish-style design with new building codes, which moved away from the flammable wood structures previously used to brick buildings and the introduction of tile roofs, iron railings, and balconies. These new materials were less flammable, which was a good thing, as it took several decades longer before a volunteer fire department was firmly established in the city.

Alongside the firemen tombs are other notable groups, including the Soon On Tong Association, where the immigrant Chinese community buried their loved ones. This tomb contains a fireplace, where pieces of paper with names of the deceased are written down and then placed into the fire for their spirits to be released and take flight into the heavens.

Paranormal activity in this cemetery includes reports of smelling smoke but never seeing a fire, as well as photographs taken at the tombs, only to see faces appear in the photos where no one was standing. Other eyewitnesses report seeing bits of paper flying around on fire, like the papers burnt at the Chinese tomb. According to the reports, on some full moon evenings, the papers can be seen flying around for a moment on fire and, instead of burning to ash, then take the shape of tiny birds and fly away.

3. Odd Fellows Rest

A variety of fruit trees including orange, grapefruit, and peach trees, grows inside Odd Fellows Cemetery. Like the Greek story of Demeter and Persephone, local lore says not to eat the fruit from these trees or else you'll be trapped in a contractual agreement with the underworld.

Founded in 1847 by The Independent Order of Odd Fellows, a secret society that dates back to ancient Rome, this cemetery has a large number of poetic inscriptions placed at each tomb. The cemetery was designed in a triangular shape and includes Odd Fellow references to Egypt, including the all-seeing eye.

This cemetery is best known for the first burials presented here, which included a funeral procession led by circus bandwagons pulled by 16 horses. Currently, the cemetery has fallen into a state of decay, as it appears that there is no longer an active Odd Fellows Lodge in the city. The cemetery is considered to be very haunted, and locals claim that one does not even need to venture inside the cemetery to experience the spectral activity.

Cabdrivers and pedestrians both report seeing a man running out of the cemetery at all hours of the night. He dashes into the street, causing taxi drivers to hit the brakes to avoid hitting the man, only to see his ghostly form disappear in front of their eyes. Inside the cemetery, visitors report seeing a large number of ghostly dogs and cats running through the grounds. An elderly gentleman is also reported to hang around just outside the cemetery walking his dog. Both the man and the dog appear in their ghostly forms, still enjoying their walks together in the afterlife. This ghost is reported to be very friendly and helpful. He often appears to people warning them that trouble is nearby and encourages them to leave the area immediately.

4, 5, AND 6. ST. PATRICK CEMETERY #1, #2, AND #3

Built as the resting place for the Irish immigrants who came to New Orleans to escape the potato famine in Ireland, St. Patrick Cemetery consists of three burial grounds labeled simply as #1, #2, and #3. St. Patrick Cemetery #3 is considered to be the most paranormally active of the three. The Irish who moved to Louisiana were not prepared for the high humidity and oppressive heat. The climate was difficult for them to physically adjust to, and they had some of the worst jobs in the city, which included digging the New Basin Canal that was filled with mosquitoes carrying yellow fever. Many of the Irish workers quickly succumbed to yellow fever and died in record numbers as the disease swept across the city.

Ghost photos and EVPs are reportedly successful in capturing activity in this cemetery more than any other area in the city. One of the reasons that so many cemeteries in New Orleans are haunted may have to do with the sweeping epidemics that went through the city in the 1840s, when St. Patrick Cemetery was founded. Common diseases included yellow fever and cholera, and people died in such high numbers that it was difficult for the living to keep up with the burials. Many of the afflicted died in a state of high fever and pain. In these instances, psychics, mediums, and paranormal researchers who connect with these spirits find that the ghosts are unaware that they have died. These ghosts hover in a timeless state, where they believe they have just awoken from their fever and wonder why they are not back at their home. Because of this misunderstanding, these ghosts are at unrest in large numbers, which has led to the numerous reports of ghostly sightings and voices heard from men, women, and children calling out to their loved ones from the grave.

7. Charity Hospital Cemetery

Founded in 1847, Charity Hospital Cemetery was a mass gravesite created to bury thousands of poverty-stricken patients who died from the epidemics of cholera and yellow fever. The gravesites are unmarked, and there may be up to 150,000 people buried here. Up until a few years ago, the only eerie testament and memorial to the dead buried here was a large cross and sign posted in 1989 from Tulane University and LSU Medical School thanking those who donated their bodies to scientific research. The ashes from those who donated their bodies to the medical schools are scattered here on the grounds.

Gruesome local reports and stories state that wild dogs have been running through the cemetery for years. Reportedly the animals dig up bones and body parts and carry them off. Barbed-wire fencing was installed to stop these desecrations.

Interestingly, with all the horrifically sad stories of the people who suffered and then were buried here, there were not many reports of haunted activity until the past decade. In 2002, city officials looked into removing the bodies from the cemetery to take over the land and build a bus stop in its place. There was a large public outcry against the idea, but officials continued to push for the demolition and assigned a team of archeologists to investigate what the cost would be to move the occupants from the cemetery.

As the burial grounds were being disturbed each day by the archeological teams, locals began to report hearing strange screams and moaning coming from the cemetery at all hours of the night. Ghosts in hospital patient gowns began to be seen running through the cemetery and into the streets, scaring drivers and pedestrians alike. The cemetery had been closed and locked up prior to this time, but as the paranormal activity increased each evening, tales soon swept the city. The project was then canceled. An announcement from city officials stated that they had decided to abandon the project due to the cost of the project along with the unpopularity of the idea by locals.

Left abandoned again, the Charity Hospital Cemetery was recently reopened to the public after two monuments were placed on the grounds dedicated to victims of Hurricane Katrina. The first monument reads: "This memorial honors those who perished as a result of Hurricane Katrina, August 29, 2005. This storm led to both the greatest natural and greatest man-made disaster in our nation's history. This memorial provides a final resting place for those whose bodies remain unidentified and unclaimed. May they have eternal peace. It also serves as a tribute to survivors and their work to rebuild New Orleans and their lives."

The second monument marker reads: "More than 1,100 persons in New Orleans and the surrounding communities perished in the wake of Hurricane Katrina. An unprecedented effort to recover and identify the dead was carried out. Dr. Frank Minyard, Coroner of Orleans Parish, created the New Orleans Katrina Memorial to build a final resting place to honor those victims who remain unidentified or unclaimed. The memorial received the remains of the unidentified and unclaimed victims and was dedicated to their memory on August 29, 2008. May they and other victims of Hurricane Katrina find eternal peace." Reportedly an angel statue will also be erected between the two monument markers as a symbol of peace and healing for the city.

Interestingly, once the project was abandoned to destroy the cemetery, the haunting activity immediately ceased. This has led many to speculate that those who are buried here are again resting in peace and that they will only rise to protect their final resting place from destruction.

8. St. John/Hope Mausoleum

Originally established in 1867 as a Protestant cemetery by the St. John Evangelical Lutheran Church, the cemetery was later sold in 1929 to John Huber, who built the Hope Mausoleum in 1931 and opened the cemetery to burials of all faiths. The most notable and distinguishing features of the Hope Mausoleum are the stained glass windows featuring landmarks of New Orleans, including Jackson Square and the Cabildo, along with four striking stained glass windows showcasing the four seasons.

The majority of the supernatural reports at this location come from inside the Hope Mausoleum. The reports state that in the halls you will meet many of the deceased residents buried here, appearing in full apparition, engaged in deep conversations with each other. While startling at first to see or overhear, eyewitnesses claim that the ghosts are friendly as they continue on with their conversations. The only time they appear to be annoyed is when someone attempts to interrupt their chat, at which time they give a haughty look and then disappear from sight. It is customary for families over multiple generations to be buried together in these tombs, so perhaps the family ties that bind and long-term friendships and relationships continue indefinitely here in the spirit world.

9 and 10. Dispersed of Judah/ Chevra Thilim and Gates of Prayer

This Jewish cemetery was founded in 1846 by Judah Touro. The haunting reports found here are the lowest in number compared to other surrounding cemeteries. Most visitors report a feeling of being watched, but the ghost or entity never appears as an apparition. Voices are heard whispering and are said to be carried through the wind both here and in the adjoining Chevra Thilim, a small triangular piece of land attached to the Dispersed of Judah cemetery, founded in 1973. Chevra Thilim is rare in the fact that the burials are belowground with headstones on the tomb in uniformity. The Jewish cemetery stands out in its simplicity and lack of ornate decor.

Nearby, Gates of Prayer #1, founded in 1853, is also a final resting place for the Jewish community.

11. MASONIC CEMETERY

Established in 1865 by the Masonic Fraternity Grand Lodge of the state of Louisiana, the Masonic Cemetery is one of the most private cemeteries in the city. Facing City Park Avenue, the cemetery is filled with Masonic symbols and monuments, including the Gothic-inspired Perfect Union Lodge Tomb, where the roof is accessible by an outside stairway. Masons were very active in New Orleans, and reportedly the beloved Catholic priest Pere Antoine de Sedella was a Mason. His spirit is most often seen near St. Louis Cathedral rather than the cemetery.

The Masonic Cemetery is described as the calmest and most restful cemetery in the city. It is always peaceful and well-maintained, though occasionally graffiti in the form of occult symbols are reportedly found drawn near some graves, as some people attempt to connect to the spirit world by asking the assistance of the Masons. The supernatural sightings reported here include seeing Masons walking up and down the stairs at twilight and at midnight to stand on the rooftop of the Perfect Union Lodge Tomb. They are said to silently climb the stairs and then stand together looking up at the stars.

Other sightings include seeing and hearing the ghosts of a group of jolly riverboat captains who love to sing. They often appear in the vicinity of the tomb dedicated to the Red River

Pilots, an association of steamboat captains. Most assume the captains are still enjoying their time together swapping stories, gambling, playing cards, and enjoying a song and a drink together during moonlit evenings.

12. Holt Cemetery

Established in 1879, Holt Cemetery is a demure burial ground with little traditional architectural fanfare. Designated for the indigents of New Orleans, it is completely understandable given the economic situation of the families buried here that their greatest concern was not to build luxurious monuments for their graves. With that in mind, though, Holt is quite different in comparison to the Charity Hospital Cemetery. Though both are resting places for poverty-stricken people, Holt families claimed their deceased loved ones and had them buried here, while at Charity many of the bodies went unclaimed and, in some cases, unnamed.

What is fascinating at Holt is that the love of family is omnipresent here at the cemetery. Many of the burial sites are lovingly decorated in a wide variety of artistic expressions. The sites are colorful, decorated with flowers, stones, cherubs, and odds and ends that have specific meanings, many times understood only by family members. Many relatives find it comforting to visit the gravesites of their loved ones here and tend to the graves on a frequent basis. Some locals disagree that the cemetery is beautiful in its own way with these unique family designs on each site. Others, though, fully appreciate the loving care emotionally expressed at each site, which might be best described as folk art, with hand-painted signs and artwork.

Holt is known for being one of the most active cemeteries for Voodoo rituals, and all sorts of paraphernalia used for various rituals are routinely found throughout the cemetery. The graves here are underground, and many of the plots have a sunken-in appearance, and some are covered with stones and handmade markers. This view—along with the accompanying Spanish moss dripping from the trees, gravestones tilting on their sides, and some gravesites twisting and lurching back into the earth—gives the site the appearance of a haunted cemetery straight out of Hollywood.

It is also the burial site of legendary jazz musician Buddy Bolden, who is in an unmarked grave somewhere in the cemetery. Buddy is considered to be the undisputed king of jazz and is revered by musicians around the world. Sadly, he was overcome by schizophrenia and was placed in a mental asylum until his death. He was buried as a pauper in Holt Cemetery with no headstone. In 1998, a marker was dedicated to him at the cemetery in respect and admiration. Séances are reportedly held each year in the cemetery by a group of people who attempt to contact this world-famous musician to determine where he is buried on the grounds.

The ghostly appearances in Holt Cemetery are most often experienced and reported by the families who frequently visit the gravesites of their loved ones buried here. They report a comforting feeling and presence of their ancestors as they visit with them. They often spend hours here discussing family news and updating them on what's going on in the world.

13. GREENWOOD CEMETERY

Established in 1852 by the Fireman's Charitable and Benevolent Association, Greenwood Cemetery is more than 150 acres in size. In distinctive comparison to the other cemeteries in the city, a wall does not surround Greenwood Cemetery. It is open to public view and is the home to many society tombs, including the Protective Order of the Elks Society, along with many firemen tombs and Civil War soldiers. Averaging more than a thousand burials each year, it is said to be the most active cemetery in current use in the area.

With a wide variety of decorated tombs and vaults to peruse, it's the openness of Greenwood that many find so appealing. Ghost reports run the gamut here, from ghost pets to crying baby ghosts, Civil War soldiers, loving ghost couples taking romantic walks and holding hands until they disappear in the moonlight, ghost children playing games of chase, and, most notably, the ghost of John Kennedy Toole, a graduate of Tulane University and university professor. Toole wrote *A Confederacy of Dunces*, which he attempted to have published in 1969. Distraught over his inability to find a publisher for his book, Toole is reported to have committed suicide in despair at the age of 31. In 1980, Louisiana State University published his book, and he was posthumously awarded a Pulitzer Prize in 1981. The ghost of John Kennedy Toole reportedly appears to students when they visit the cemetery. If they listen closely, he often will share a joke or offer advice on writing.

KALA'S TRAVEL TIPS

- Portals are energized by actions surrounding the area. There is a distinct feeling and **energetic vibration at the crossroads of City Park Avenue and Canal Street.** For decades spiritual practices occurred at Congo Square, and, along with the amount of cemeteries in close proximity, this history creates a vortex that can be felt by anyone with psychic sensitivities.

- These cemeteries are works of art in their own right, with stunning architecture and testimony to the love and care our ancestors created in these cities of the dead. They are wonderful to visit for the historical as well as the supernatural experiences. However, most of these areas are not safe to visit alone, not due to the paranormal entities but rather due to the very human criminal element in the city. **It is best to visit each of these cemeteries in large groups,** accompanied by local tour guides who know the routes and provide safe journeys through the cities of the dead. Please note that after-hours entry into the cemeteries is punishable by law, and you can be arrested. Removal of any artifacts from the cemeteries, as well as marking on any tomb, is also illegal.

- Several cemeteries here are counted as a part of a group rather than individually. Chevra Thilim, for example, is relatively new, founded in 1973, and is considered to be part of the Dispersed of Judah rather than being counted as a cemetery on its own. **Local legends believe that it was the original cemeteries established here that created the portal to the underworld** rather than the recent additions.

- **Beware of the old woman ghost** with long white hair, who is said to be insatiably curious when you are ghost-hunting in St. Patrick Cemetery #3. The legends state that she has been known to attach herself to visitors and follow them around for hours, if not days. Zombie sightings are also frequently reported in this cemetery.

Jean Lafitte's Infamous Pirate Bar

"Times are not good here. The city is crumbling into ashes. It has been buried under taxes and frauds and maladministrations so that it has become a study for archaeologists. . . . But it is better to live here in sackcloth and ashes, than to own the whole State of Ohio."
—Lafcadio Hearn, *The Life and Letters of Lafcadio Hearn, Vol. 1*

IN NORTH CAROLINA, children grow up hearing the swashbuckling tales of Blackbeard the Pirate. In Louisiana, the children are regaled with the adventures of Jean Lafitte, the most famous pirate in New Orleans.

Jean and his brother Pierre were believed to be Frenchmen who migrated to Port-au-Prince, Haiti, in search of their fortunes, which then led them to Cuba. It is believed that around 1806, as Spanish ships were delivering goods to New Orleans, the brothers saw the easy prey and decided to follow these treasures to Louisiana. Once they arrived, they set up their pirating headquarters on two barrier islands located along the southwestern Louisiana coast called Grand Isle and Grand Terre.

By 1811, the Lafitte brothers had established a firm stronghold in the area, and the dashing Jean became known the Pirate King of New Orleans. Jean and his brother were very popular among the Creole people, as they were able to procure almost any item that the locals desired from France or other locations on demand. In addition, the brothers Lafitte reportedly employed more than a thousand people throughout the area,

Still standing as it was more than 150 years ago, Lafitte's Bar is a great place to get a drink and mix with locals.

who worked as pirates, sailors, dockworkers, distributors, store clerks, purveyors, and security who worked the docks as well as moved goods from the pirate ships into local stores to sell them expediently. Jean ran the seafaring business of pirating with his ships, and Pierre ran the store and supervised the employees who moved and sold the goods.

Handsome and charming, Jean spoke English, French, Spanish, and Italian and has been described as a well-dressed man who was 6 foot, 2 inches tall with dark hair and a mustache. He made friends easily and was well respected; he was seen as a romantic figure by women and an impressive business entrepreneur by men, who referred to him as a privateer and captain rather than as a pirate. Rather than being seen as a scoundrel or scallywag, most of the Creoles saw Jean as an entrepreneur, who, for the right price, could get them almost anything they desired.

In 1812, the United States was preparing for war against Britain, and the importation of foreign goods was forbidden. The

French Creoles did not want to be inconvenienced by this block-ade of goods from Europe. In answer to their call, Jean Lafitte became a Santa Claus figure of sorts who delivered goods that were not attainable in any legal manner during this time. It is said that by 1813, almost every store in New Orleans stocked goods from the Lafitte brothers. Store owners who did not buy goods from the Lafittes suffered, as they could not acquire many of these in-demand goods legitimately, nor could they compete against the Lafitte price discounts.

Almost anything could be found stored at Barataria, the name Lafitte gave to his base of operations on the barrier islands. Some locals ventured out to Grand Isle to shop directly from the ships as the goods were pulled off the ships. Inventory often included medicine, maps, tools, weapons, fine silks and clothes, exotic spices, jewelry, trunks, wine and rum, furniture, and any other goods you can imagine. Others shopped in New Orleans at the store operated by Pierre Lafitte, where the prices were so reasonable that shoppers filled the stores daily. The Lafitte brothers were doing so well that they were able to open lines of credit to the locals so they could shop at will.

The Lafitte brothers were held in high regard in the Creole community and were always invited to the social events and balls each year. Jean also built a mansion at Barataria, where he entertained and threw parties each year; he also enter-tained at his impressive home in the French Quarter, where his brother also lived.

Business continued to boom for the Lafitte brothers even as Spanish diplomats continued to complain about the lack of protection for their ships from pirate attacks. As mentioned pre-viously in chapter three, this eventually forced the governor of Louisiana to take some form of action and arrest Pierre for mov-ing stolen goods. In 1814, the British were advancing on the United States and heading toward New Orleans. If the British took control of this port, they would be able to block all goods and services that floated down from the cities along the Mississippi River, which would severely cripple the United States. Requiring all the resources he could gather to win this fight, General Andrew Jackson agreed to have Pierre released from prison and asked Jean and almost 400 men from his pirate army to help fight the British.

Jackson knew this was instrumental in saving the city of New Orleans, as the pirates were well-armed, fierce fighters who knew the area better than anyone else and knew how to skirt around the barrier islands and hide in the swamps. They knew the weather patterns and the shifting tides, and they were experts in sneak attacks.

This partnership also had an unexpected side effect with a considerable bonus. The French Creoles, realizing that their city was now under the grave reality of becoming owned and operated by the British, rallied under the announcement that their beloved Jean Lafitte was going to fight with the Americans. Word had spread that Jean had turned down a very generous offer of compensation, that is a bribe, from the British, which reportedly was the sum of $30,000 in gold, along with a full pardon and the title of captain in the British Navy, should he choose to fight for the British.

His patriotism for New Orleans, which most likely was linked to his personal business ambitions, rallied the Creoles to take action and support the United States in the war. This was the first time in the Creole community that a sense of American patriotism, rather than French or New Orleanian patriotism, had been awakened. While this may seem surprising to some, it is important to remember that Louisiana was a territory owned by the French and Spanish off and on. Becoming part of the United States was relatively new at this time. The rest, as they say, is history, as Lafitte, his band of pirates, and the troops

Side entrance to Lafitte's Bar

led by General Andrew Jackson were victorious in defeating the British and sending them on the run.

Before and after the battle against the British, Jean and Pierre operated a store on Royal Street, where they sold their goods. They had also established a blacksmith shop on St. Philip Street, which some say did technically operate as a blacksmith shop, but the main purpose was to smuggle the goods. It is here at the blacksmith shop, the only remaining property standing of the Lafittes, where dead men do tell tales in their ghostly forms.

Jean Lafitte's Blacksmith Shop, originally built in 1722, is now referred to as Jean Lafitte's Blacksmith Shop Bar. It is one of the oldest standing structures in the French Quarter and also one of the few remaining French architectural-style structures that survived the Great Fires of New Orleans in 1788 and 1794, which destroyed most of the buildings in the quarter.

In a bar this old, it's very likely that the bartenders have been serving both spirits and humans over the years. Many people claim to see the ghost of Jean Lafitte walking through the bar in a pirate-style hat speaking with several men who appear to be part of his pirate crew. Local lore says that if you want to make the ghost of Jean appear, speak in a whisper about the rumors that pirate treasure is still hidden here in the blacksmith shop, and he will appear to protect his treasure still hidden somewhere in New Orleans.

Locals also report seeing ghostly apparitions near the fireplace, which was once used for blacksmithing. The majority of ghostly sightings and reports are not of pirates but rather of bar patrons who frequented here for years. After they died, it appears they prefer to enjoy another drink at the tavern rather than moving on into spirit world. For some, New Orleans truly is heavenly, and there is no desire to leave, even after death.

I heard these stories from many locals here in the city, and in the interest of research, I spent a good amount of time at the bar to see what stories and legends prevail. I have it on good account, told to me in confidence by one of the tour guides in New Orleans, that there was a guide who so loved this bar that he made the other guides promise that upon his death, he would be cremated and some of his ashes would be sprinkled outside at Jean Lafitte's. They assured me that they did indeed sprinkle a few of his ashes when no one was looking, and I am sworn to secrecy of when and how this occurred. After this incident, the guides began seeing their deceased friend standing at the bar, and he regularly appears at the bar when they are there.

While visiting Jean Lafitte's Bar, I was swept away by the energy of the place. Any building this old holds a lot of energy from the people who have been inside throughout the years. Even when you pass by the tavern, the people sitting inside by the windows have a haunting energy about them. There's an air about the place that seems to affect some people when they go inside to drink. They appear to become like pirates, keeping a watchful eye on the place and ready to pounce out of their hiding place at a moment's notice should the pirate's call be heard.

The bar is dark, and when I visited, it was very busy. Because of this, I would have been hard-pressed to discern who was very much alive and who was in ghost form. I spent most of my time here in conversation with locals to hear their ghost stories and experiences in the bar, of which there are literally hundreds.

I didn't see a ghost while at the bar, though the ambience certainly lends itself to being a haunted space, and I certainly enjoyed the spirits. I tend to agree with local reports that the bar is haunted more by deceased patrons who want to enjoy one more night at the bar rather than by the pirates themselves. After exploring the history of Jean Lafitte, it seems much more likely that he would haunt the barrier islands of Grand Isle and Grand Terre, doing what he most loved to do.

⚜ KALA'S TRAVEL TIPS

• If you want to hang with the locals, **catch a Saints game at Jean Lafitte's Bar,** where you'll hear what's really going on in the city. Try the Voodoo Daiquiris, which are made with fruit juice and are much tastier than some other places on Bourbon. They are so delicious that I've been known to try many of them for research purposes.

• Some people report seeing **red eyes** floating over the fireplace area inside the bar. There are also tales of a woman who appears in a mirror. The charming bar is lit by candlelight, and you'll feel transported back in time. Anyone with psychic abilities will pick up on the energy of the place. Paranormal researchers also come away with a variety of orbs and mists appearing in their photos.

• Legend has it that General Andrew Jackson and Jean Lafitte planned the Battle of New Orleans while sipping on absinthe cocktails at the **Absinthe House** on the corner of Bienville and Bourbon. The Absinthe House did not become a public saloon until 1826; up until this time it was a private dwelling, but the legend states that the two men met there and were served drinks by the private owner of this residence.

CHAPTER 15

More Than 200 Years of Spirits at the Napoleon House

"I'm not going to try to lay down in words the lure of this place. Every great writer in the land, from Faulkner to Twain to Rice to Ford, has tried to do it and fallen short. It is impossible to capture the essence, tolerance, and spirit of south Louisiana in words and to try is to roll down a road of clichés, bouncing over beignets and beads and brass bands and it just is what it is. It is home."

—Chris Rose, *1 Dead in Attic*

IF NAPOLEON BONAPARTE could have finished his bucket list before his death, a visit to New Orleans would most assuredly have been on his list. Though he was unable to reside here in the city, his spirit and legacy left a strong impression.

Growing up in Louisiana, children are quickly introduced to Napoleon in elementary school, as the state of Louisiana operates under Napoleonic law. This differs from the legal system operating elsewhere in the United States, which is based on British common law with some adaptations. The French influence is present throughout the state, including the state being divided legally into parishes rather than counties. Napoleon's legacy can be found throughout New Orleans, including a variety of streets named after his famous battles and conquests.

When Napoleon was captured and imprisoned on the Isle of Saint Helena, a group of Frenchmen in New Orleans began to plan his rescue. They decided to acquire a yacht and sail to the Isle of Saint Helena, where they would participate in a daring rescue

The Napoleon House

of Napoleon and bring him to New Orleans to live out the rest of his life. One of the men involved with this plan was Nicholas Girod, the mayor of New Orleans from 1812 to 1815. Girod offered his home to Napoleon to live in upon his rescue. Many meetings regarding the rescue attempt were discussed here at Girod's home, which began to be referred to as the Napoleon House.

Unfortunately, Napoleon died on the Isle of Saint Helena before the men could rescue him. Some reports state that he died from stomach cancer, but the most popular opinion is that he was poisoned by arsenic, which gave the appearance of stomach cancer.

Even after the death of Napoleon, the Girod House kept its nickname of the Napoleon House. For more than 200 years it has served locals and travelers alike with food and drink, while maintaining its historical significance. Regarding the haunted history of the house, more people are apt to tell you that it has been haunted more by living artists and writers, including Tom

Piazza, Andrei Codrescu, Richard Ford, Julie Smith, and Robert Olen Butler, especially during the 20th century. It is said that the writers and artists find the timelessness of the place charming and as close to bohemian Paris as one can find in the United States.

As for ghostly sightings, it's never been Mayor Girod or Napoleon who haunt the home. During the Civil War, the second floor of the house operated as an infirmary, and many soldiers died in the house during this time. Ghostly apparitions of soldiers are the ones most often seen on the second story, and there are also reports of hearing boots pacing back and forth on the floor.

As a writer, Napoleon House was on my own personal bucket list. I had been by the house many times, sometimes on foot and other times by carriage ride, as this location and Jean Lafitte's Blacksmith Shop Bar are on every tour ride in the city. I had often looked at the peeling plaster walls, viewed patrons munching on muffuletta sandwiches, and wished I had the time to stop in and become part of the scenery myself. This time I resolved that I would make the time to visit and soak up the atmosphere. As I entered the bar, I was greeted by some of the friendliest bartenders in town, and local patrons were happy to share the history of the house. None of the staff had a particularly wild story to share about a haunting in the house, but some had ghost stories to share about somewhere they had been in New Orleans where they did see or sense a ghost. Hauntings in this city are as common as good drinks, both of which can be found in plentiful numbers everywhere.

Some of the locals who attended private parties here, held on the second floor of the house, shared their paranormal experiences with me. While most did not see a ghost up there, they all described a similar feeling of being watched by a presence lurking in the corner to observe the ongoing festivities.

THE DEATH MASK OF NAPOLEON

Creation of the Mask

Doctor Francesco Antommarchi, one of Napoleon's physician at the time of his death, is believed to have crafted the original mold for this mask forty hours after Napoleon died on May 5, 1821. The mold was later used to cast four bronze masks, including this one, and three replicas.

Some experts discount Antommarchi's role, claiming that another of Napoleon's physicians, Francis Burton, created the mask. Others believe that the mold is not of Napoleon's face, but that of François Eugène Robeaud, who occasionally doubled for the emperor.

Presentation to New Orleans

Doctor Antommarchi presented Napoleon's death mask to the city of New Orleans shortly after he settled here in 1834. City officials displayed the mask in the Cabildo, along with instruments Antommarchi had used to conduct Napoleon's autopsy. Antommarchi practiced medicine in New Orleans until 1838, when he moved to Mexico.

Further Adventures of the Mask

City authorities moved the death mask, along with their offices, from the Cabildo to Gallier Hall in 1853. After the mask disappeared during the Civil War, a former city treasurer spotted it in a junk wagon as it was being hauled to the dump in 1866. Rather than return it to the city, he took it home and put it on display there. Eventually, the death mask wound up in the Atlanta home of Louisiana native Captain William Greene Raoul, president of the Mexican National Railroad.

Return to New Orleans

Napoleon's death mask made its way back to the Crescent City in 1909 after Captain Raoul read a newspaper article about the missing mask. He wrote to the mayor of the mask's whereabouts and donated it to New Orleans, which in turn transferred it to the Louisiana State Museum.

The Louisiana State Museum at the Cabildo has a death mask of Napoleon on display.

While in the house, I could easily see why so many writers enjoy spending time here. It's easy to conjure up a muse to help with any type of writing in this space. The walls seep with energy from thousands of conversations over the years, and the atmosphere is like being in Old Europe, as if stepping back in time. One feels as though he or she has stepped into a novel by simply entering the building. It's enough to break through any writer's block and stir the creative juices to flow freely again.

The hauntings at the Napoleon House may not be as rich in the traditional style of ghosts as it is at other locations in the quarter, but the spirit of the place is rich beyond compare. The energy here provides a unique ability to stir up creative ideas and put them into motion. Writers from all over the world travel each year to New Orleans looking for inspiration. Should they wish to meet their muse and engage with the spirit of the city, their journey begins at the Napoleon House.

Kala's Travel Tips

- As was custom in his time, a death mask was made of Napoleon's face, from which four bronzes and three replicas were made. In the **Cabildo museum in New Orleans,** one of the bronze death masks, given to the city as a gift from Napoleon's personal physician, Dr. Antommarchi, can be seen.

- **Beethoven** was a fan of Napoleon and composed "Eroiqua" in honor of Napoleon. You can hear this classical music still played today in the Napoleon House.

- Try the **Pimm's Cup drink,** a gin-based drink, while at the Napoleon House. This is a secret recipe, and it's tradition to have one. The **Sazeracs** made here are wonderful as well. You can buy the mixes to make Pat O'Brien's hurricanes and Pimm's Cup at home, but everyone says (and I've tried it myself and agree) that they never taste the same at home like they do while in New Orleans. So it's best to leave the making of these cocktails to the professionals.

- The Napoleon House has appeared in movies, including *The Curious Case of Benjamin Button* and *Runaway Jury.*

CHAPTER 16

Gourmet Ghosts Love Antoine's and Arnaud's Restaurants

"At least once a day . . . one should throw all care to the winds, relax completely, and dine leisurely and well."

—Count Arnaud Cazenave

TO DINE IN NEW ORLEANS is to embrace the culinary roots of multiple cultures, which extend far beyond the proverbial gumbo. One could literally spend months in the city at a different establishment every night and never eat the same meal twice.

The food itself is a spiritual experience. It's no surprise in a city like New Orleans that some people enjoy their favorite restaurants to such a high degree that they don't allow an inconvenient situation like death to end their good times. In the city where the motto is *laissez les bon temps rouler* ("let the good times roll"), it quite possibly is one of the most pleasant places to remain in the afterlife, enjoying the music, Mardi Gras, and of course, the food.

Almost every restaurant in town has at least one ghost story to share, but for this tale I'm going to share with you two of my favorite restaurants in the French Quarter, both of which have more than their share of supernatural experiences and adventures.

ANTOINE'S

Antoine's is a family-owned restaurant that opened in 1840 and has been offering exemplary service and French Creole

Entrance to Antoine's

cuisine since its inception. With more than 14 dining rooms, the restaurant is capable of holding up to 700 guests at a time. Several of the dining rooms are named after the Carnival krewes, which include Rex, Proteus, and the 12th Night Revelers. A krewe is an organization or club that puts on a parade or special event during Carnival. My favorite is the Rex Room; the king of Rex reigns over Mardi Gras each year.

I grew up listening to my parents talking about their dinners here with friends and dreamed of the day when I would be able to dress up and dine at Antoine's while sipping a French 75 cocktail. The restaurant is so romantic, and the fact that it is fifth-generation family-owned is especially touching, knowing that a family legacy was created through a ton of hard work and the desire to provide the best food and service.

In the modern world where restaurants close within a few years and chain eateries microwave food and call it dinner, Antoine's is a testament to what high-quality products and

Dinner inside Antoine's

service can create and sustain, regardless of the economy and state of the world around them.

Antoine Alciatore began the restaurant in 1840 with his wife, and both were dedicated to creating a fine establishment and family legacy. In 1874, Antoine passed away, and his wife ran the restaurant while their son, Jules, went to study at a culinary school in France. When Jules returned to New Orleans, he became the chef and made his mark with the creation of Oysters Rockefeller. The restaurant continued to be passed down through the family, with Jules's son, Roy, being the next to take over.

One of the reasons that the restaurant is thought to have been so successful is the legend that every family member involved in Antoine's restaurant has encountered the ghost of Antoine in one form or another. Reportedly, he looks after the restaurant and keeps a watchful eye on the operations to ensure that the finest quality is still being preserved. Guests and some staff members have also reported seeing the ghost of Antoine. By all accounts, as long as there is an Antoine's restaurant, Antoine himself will be there to look after the staff and the guests.

His spirit is not the only ghost reported in the building. The legendary Japanese Room often has a ghost walking in and out of the room, even when the doors are locked. A young man is seen walking up to the doors and then walking right through them. When staff members investigate and open the doors, no one is inside. The Japanese Room is decorated with hand-painted walls in Oriental design. Large banquets were held in this room until December 7, 1941, when the Japanese bombed Pearl Harbor. When this occurred, Antoine's closed the room, and it remained locked for 43 years, though it did not stop the ghost of Antoine from entering and checking in on things. The room was later reopened to the public in 1984. Both the ghost of the young man and the ghost of Antoine continue to be seen walking into this room.

The appropriately named Mystery Room also has reports of ghostly sightings by a variety of spirits, including Antoine. The Mystery Room was given this name during Prohibition. Guests would go through a door in the ladies' restroom (behind Hermes Bar) and enter a secret room, where they would then exit with a coffee cup full of alcohol. When the guests would return to their tables, others would ask where they picked up the coffee cup, and they would reply, as instructed, "It's a mystery to me."

While the original entrance was near the restroom, you can now access the Mystery Room from Hermes or by going through the Large Annex Room down past the Dungeon Room through two sets of doors. The coffee cup is no longer required, as drinks are now available at your table.

ARNAUD'S

As you step off Bourbon Street and round the corner to Arnaud's, you instantly feel as if you have stepped back in time and are preparing to dine like a real Creole. Founded in 1918, a French wine salesman named Arnaud Cazena built the restaurant. A variety of private dining rooms, as well as a museum filled with New Orleans memorabilia on the second floor, are inside. The museum includes elaborate Mardi Gras costumes worn by Count Arnaud and his daughter, Germaine Wells, who reigned as queen over 22 Mardi Gras balls, more than any other woman in the history of Carnival.

There have been hundreds of paranormal sightings at the restaurant, including employees who have seen a ghostly gentleman standing near the beveled glass windows. At first the tuxedo-clad man is noticed standing alone. But once approached, he immediately disappears. Most believe that it is Count Arnaud checking in on the restaurant.

Others report seeing a woman wearing a hat exiting the ladies' room and crossing the hall, where she then walks into the wall and disappears. There have been so many reports of this sighting that investigations were held to determine the original structure and layout of the building. It was discovered that this area once had a staircase where the wall is now placed. The ghostly woman is simply walking to the stairs from the time she was here, and in her world, there is no wall there to block her entry. Some believe this ghost to be Germaine, the daughter of Arnaud, who still enjoys the restaurant as well. She reportedly also appears in the museum by her costumes and has been seen in her ghostly form at various Carnival balls each year.

Beyond the supernatural sightings reported by local diners, tourists, and waitstaff, Arnaud's reports that even its CPA experienced a ghostly visitation in the restaurant when he was alone one evening conducting inventory. While he was working, he

The corner sign points the way to Arnaud's.

noticed a strong drop in temperature in the room. As he felt the cold chill overtake him, he became aware of a presence standing behind him. Turning around, he found himself alone in the room. The CPA was in the Richelieu Bar at the time, which is one of the oldest standing structures in the restaurant, dating back to the late 1700s. In a building still standing for several centuries, there is the opportunity for a wide variety of hauntings over its incarnations. Over the years, so many different ghosts have been seen and felt at the restaurant that not all of them have been identified by name.

I once saw a ghost while dining at Arnaud's with my husband. We were enjoying dinner on a Friday evening, and the restaurant was packed to the brim and humming with conversation. As we sat at our table, I noticed that many of the surrounding tables held groups of men who were there not only to dine but also were deeply involved in discussing business. I mused that over the years there must have been thousands of

Entrance to Arnaud's

business deals conducted here at these tables over a stiff drink
and a good steak.

The restaurant just has that kind of feel about it; it's very
much a gentlemen's club–type atmosphere, where one can dis-
creetly discuss business in a civilized and elegant manner. A
large group of people was seated at tables near us, and it was easy
to tell that they had traveled to New Orleans for a conference and
had decided to enjoy the city and dine at the famous Arnaud's.
These groups did not hold my attention, but right past these
tables I saw a group of men, clearly locals, for whom Arnaud's
is not only a pastime but also a place where they belong, as an
extension of their office where they meet to seal deals and break
ground on new ventures.

These men were in deep discussion, and it was clear by
the conversation and body language that they were from two
different parties who were hoping to do business together. As

I enjoyed my people-watching, I noticed a man in a tuxedo standing behind one of the men seated at this table. I thought how odd it was that the man did not look up or inquire why the man was standing so close to him. That was until a moment later when the man disappeared completely for a moment and then reappeared. I then realized he was a ghost standing there at the table.

The ghost continued to stand behind the seated man, who continued his conversation, which appeared to be a pitch or presentation of some sort to the others at the table. He would stop on occasion to rub at his ear, as if something was buzzing near his ear and he was trying to chase it away. He continued to speak to the other men at the table, though it appeared as if the conversation was not going well. Several of the men began to sit back in their seats, while others looked down at the table and nursed their drinks. Whatever the man was saying, he certainly was not captivating their interest, and it looked as if he was losing any momentum he had gained previously in the conversation.

He began to speak louder, which did nothing to gain back control of the conversation. One of the other men touched another man's arm and pulled him to the side to speak quietly to him. From all appearances, it seemed that whatever the man was presenting, there was not going to be a sale or agreement this evening.

Looking a bit nervous, the man began rubbing his ear, and this time he looked around as if he expected to see someone standing behind him. Seeing no one there, he turned back around and took a sip of his drink. The ghost standing behind him looked at the other men and then bent down and whispered something directly into this man's ear. The man looked surprised and then had a thoughtful look on his face. He looked off into the distance as if he was having some deep new thoughts. He then began to speak to the men with what appeared to be a new approach in his conversation. His style and demeanor had changed, and he had a different air about him. The men began to nod in approval at this point and lean in to hear more of the conversation.

By the end of the dinner it appeared that the deal was done, as they were all smiles and shaking hands. I have no doubt that the ghost who whispered in this gentleman's ear gave him the information and ideas needed to complete the business deal.

I left the restaurant that evening wondering how many business deals are done each week at Arnaud's, and how many of these deals are assisted by those in spirit at each table. I hope he left him a good tip!

⚜ Kala's Travel Tips

- To be part of the in crowd **at Antoine's, ask to be seated in one of the back rooms** when calling for reservations. Otherwise you'll be seated in the front dining room, where most unsuspecting tourists dine. My favorite room is the Large Annex Room, where you become part of the tradition like other generations of families who have dined there. You'll also be dining with locals, where you'll find that most of them have had the same waiter for years and will request him each time they make a reservation. It's the custom here at Antoine's that if you enjoy a particular waiter, you can ask for his card to ensure that you can book a table with him on future visits.

- When dining at Antoine's, the waiters will recommend that you **take a tour and walk around the other rooms of the restaurant after your meal** to take in the sites of the restaurant. Take them up on this offer, as it's wonderful to see the history, including photographs of the Duke and Duchess of Windsor, Judy Garland, Pope John Paul II, Presidents Roosevelt and

Coolidge, Bob Hope, Bing Crosby, and others who dined here. This also provides a great opportunity to bump into a ghost.

• I could spend the entire chapter discussing the incredible food at each of these restaurants, but for brevity, I'll share **one of my favorite delights** from each.

At Antoine's, you must try the **Pommes de Terre Soufflés,** which are the most delightful puffed potatoes! They come out hot and puffy, and they must be eaten immediately to savor them. Once they are cooled, they are not the same, so enjoy them quickly. Antoine's is also where my husband and I had our first French 75, a cocktail named after a French World War I artillery piece, made from gin, Champagne, lemon juice, and sugar. This was the cocktail I dreamed about trying as a little girl.

At Arnaud's, I love the **Oysters Bienville** with shrimp, mushrooms, herbs, and seasonings in a white wine sauce; it's elegantly delicious and so good that as I write about this meal, I can still taste every bite as if I'm there. Oysters Rockefeller was created at Antoine's and named after J. D. Rockefeller. Oysters Bienville, on the other hand, was first created at Arnaud's. Both are divine and you must try both!

CHAPTER 17

The Enchanted Charm Gate at the Court of Two Sisters

"New Orleans food is as delicious as the less criminal forms of sin."

—Mark Twain

A Charming Entrance

The Court of Two Sisters is a restaurant in the French Quarter offering the most delightful courtyard to enjoy a meal. In the courtyard, the wisteria trees have interlocked and connected, creating a natural canopy over the courtyard that brings the space alive with sunlight peeking through the leaves. This delightful display is further highlighted by the presence of a bubbling fountain. I find wisteria to be such an interesting choice for this courtyard, as by definition, wisteria means to "cling." The wisteria canopy welcomes guests, expressing that the dining experience will offer long-lasting memories of the event.

The jazz brunch at the Court of Two Sisters is the perfect respite from an evening spent on Bourbon Street, and its strolling jazz trio lifts the heart. While experiencing brunch in this manner, one begins to muse that every meal should be this grand. The thought of a quiet meal back home sounds absolutely appalling.

The overall effect of the restaurant creates the feeling that one has just stepped into a painting. The scene is filled with old-world charm caught in a moment of boundless spring, highlighted by the tinkle of laughter coming from guests sitting at crisp white tablecloths enjoying private moments.

Stepping into this courtyard, one walks back in time, and the city outside these doors no longer exists. This is the enchantment of the courtyards designed in New Orleans, where homes were built with the courtyard in the middle so that residents could enjoy a protected and peaceful atmosphere.

The location of the restaurant has a long and illustrious history, as this section of Royal Street was originally known as Governor's Row and was home to five governors, including Sieur Etienne de Perier, the royal governor of Louisiana from 1726 to 1733.

The name Court of Two Sisters originates from the previous owners, two Creole sisters named Emma and Bertha Camors. Their shop was here on Royal Street, and they made their living providing women in New Orleans the best gowns, gloves, perfumes, and other fashion accessories. The two sisters (born in 1858 and 1860) spent their entire lives together, and according to the history and local lore, they died within months of each other and were buried side by side in 1944 at St. Louis Cemetery #3 in New Orleans. The ghosts of both sisters are often seen throughout the restaurant, both inside the building and strolling around the courtyard.

While on one of my many visits to the Court of Two Sisters, I saw a female ghost holding what appeared to be a handkerchief. I was rushing in through the door of the ladies' room on the first floor and saw a woman standing before me. I looked up and said "Excuse me," as I was worried that my rushed entrance had made her feel uncomfortable. As I looked up at her, she smiled and then faded from my view. There was no opportunity to engage with her or have any discussion. She was simply there and then gone.

Some of the most entertaining stories I have heard about the Court of Two Sisters is about the courtyard, where locals told me that they have seen fairies dancing about in the trees and around the beautiful fountain in the center of the courtyard.

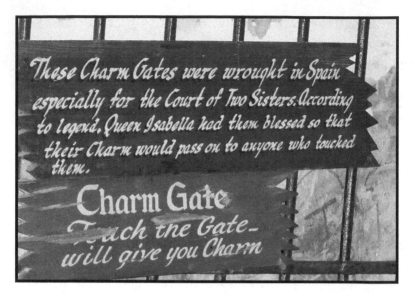

These Charm Gates were wrought in Spain especially for the Court of Two Sisters. According to legend, Queen Isabella had them blessed so that their Charm would pass on to anyone who touched them.

Charm Gate

Touch the Gate—
will give you Charm

Sign on the Charm Gates at the Court of Two Sisters

They say that you can see them day and night, and that there are many elementals, fairies, and sprites that have lived in this courtyard for hundreds of years.

I certainly agree that there is a beautiful energy here that takes you out of the mundane world and makes you truly feel transported into somewhere ethereal. This restaurant was my mother's favorite restaurant in the world, and each time she visited, she would return back home and tell me about her evening from beginning to end.

She said that every time she visited, she had a feeling that she had been there in a past life, and she would remember the man with whom she had been, whom she believed to be her husband. Each time she would dine at the restaurant, she would dream about the Court of Two Sisters later that evening. She said that in her dream she looked very similar to how she looked this lifetime, with dark brown hair and green eyes and wearing a light dove-gray dress and a cameo ring on her hand.

Many years later when she visited the Court of Two Sisters again, a gentleman friend presented her with a gift that he had purchased for her in a nearby antique shop on Royal Street earlier that day. It was an antique cameo ring, and it fit her perfectly. She was in shock, as it looked identical to the ring she had seen in her dreams, and now here it was on her hand at the very restaurant where she had dreamed that she wore this ring before.

Her friend had never heard her speak about the dream to him, nor had she ever mentioned a ring of this type to anyone. Years later she showed me the ring and explained how special it was to her in this lifetime. She felt that it was her ring from another lifetime and that it had found its way back to her again. She said that it had been charmed and carried an old spell in it that the owner of the ring would always find their way back to New Orleans.

My mother asked her friend where he had bought the ring, and he took her to the shop the next day. While she was there, she asked the owner where he had purchased the ring. He told her that a man from New York had entered his shop wanting to sell the ring. He had said that it was from his mother's estate and that she had specified in her will that the ring must be returned to New Orleans upon her death. The man from New York was unsure of what that meant exactly, so he traveled to New Orleans. He first offered the ring to a museum, which declined the offer, and so he sold it to the antiques store on Royal Street. The ring had been at the store for a couple of years, and the owner said that many people had commented on it, but none had been interested in purchasing it until my mother's friend had dropped in the day before.

My mother later passed this ring on to me, telling me that she knew that no matter where else I traveled or lived, Louisiana was always in my heart and the land I call home. It is a special treasure to me, and every time I pull it out, I swear I can hear

**Touch the Charm Gate
sign to receive good luck.**

a siren song from the muses of New Orleans calling me back home to Louisiana.

The ring sits here with me now as I write, and she appears to be shining brighter than usual, as if aware that I am telling her story now here on paper. Curious about its origin, I recently had it appraised and was told that it dates back to the Victorian times. It is the most interesting piece, as I have seen many cameo brooches, but a ring the size of a brooch is quite distinctive.

Rings, like other objects, can be charmed and have spells put on them. The energy in this ring feels as strong today as the day decades ago when my mother first showed the ring to me. I know that if I place it on my hand, I'll soon be called back to New Orleans, as its energy is so strong.

Like the ring, the charm of the two sisters and their courtyard are delightful on their own. There's true magic to be found at this location in the courtyard with the fairies and elementals, as well as at the entrance of the restaurant on Royal Street.

Waiting for you at the entrance of the Court of Two Sisters are charm gates, given to the two sisters by Queen Isabella of Spain in 1832. These gates were blessed with magic and are reported to be lucky. It is said that if you touch them, you will be the recipient of their charms. Of course the first thing I had to do when I first saw these gates was to place both hands firmly upon them to tap into the energy, as well as to tune in to what energy had been collected by the gates over the years. As a psychic with the added ability of psychometry, I can touch an object and see an experience that stayed with the object. I was very interested in seeing what stories the gates had to tell.

The iron on the gate was cool to the touch, and the restaurant has attached small blue lights to it, which drape around the gate. Standing there in front of the gate, I gripped the iron and felt a cool breeze rush past me, giving me a slight chill. As I held on to the gate, I closed my eyes and could hear past conversations from the mists of time. At first there was the energetic download of hundreds of conversations that have been collected, and then I began to see the young girls. Over the years, hundreds, maybe thousands, of young women have touched these gates, with their wish being to find true love. More than any of the other hands that have touched these gates hoping for thousands of favors and wishes to be granted, it is the wishes of the young girls that have left the strongest impression on these charmed gates. It appears that the purpose of the gates is to help people find true love.

If you are looking for a place to get engaged, have a wedding reception, or celebrate an anniversary, I believe that the Court of Two Sisters is one of the most magical and enchanted sites in which to conduct such a ceremony or celebration.

Begin by touching the charmed gate and then entering the enchanting courtyard, where the elementals await your presence, ready to delight all of your senses and provide you with a romantic atmosphere to remember for a lifetime.

If you can't wait until your next visit to New Orleans and the Court of Two Sisters to tap into this ancient energy, simply place your hand on the charm gate photo shown here and allow the charm to pass through to you.

The magic has just begun, and if the enchanted ring I'm wearing while writing this story has any say, you'll soon be on your way to visit New Orleans and the Court of Two Sisters and its charmed gates.

Kala's Travel Tips

- The **courtyard is best enjoyed in spring, fall, or winter.** Summer is a bit too warm for some to enjoy sitting outdoors, though on early mornings I find it delightful in summer too.

- Try drinking a **Sazerac,** one of the oldest cocktails in New Orleans, from the bar.

- Most of the meals are served as a buffet, and unless you're from Louisiana, you may not recognize some of the dishes prepared. It's OK. **Be adventurous**—you might like something new. If you don't, that's OK too, as there's plenty to sample and enjoy.

- **Save room for bananas Foster,** a must-have for dessert.

- The **Jazz Trio Brunch** is served daily and is a wonderful way to recover from a long evening spent on Bourbon Street.

- The restaurant is located on **Royal Street,** which is also home to many wonderful antiques shops. While you're there, try your luck and explore some of these shops; perhaps you'll find a charmed ring of your own.

- One of my favorite stores in New Orleans is **Toulouse Royale,** conveniently located on Royal Street near the Court of Two Sisters restaurant. Treasures that I have purchased here include Gaston, my beloved alligator that was created by one of the artists in New Orleans who makes the Mardi Gras floats each year. Gaston is gorgeous in an alligator-at-the-party sort of way, and he is signed by the artist. Each time I visit the city, I make sure to visit this store to discover what new delights are waiting for me.

CHAPTER 18

Gunshots and Ghosts at the Beauregard–Keyes House

"Louisiana in September was like an obscene phone call from nature. The air—moist, sultry, secretive, and far from fresh—felt as if it were being exhaled into one's face. Sometimes it even sounded like heavy breathing. Honeysuckle, swamp flowers, magnolia, and the mystery smell of the river scented the atmosphere, amplifying the intrusion of organic sleaze. It was aphrodisiac and repressive, soft and violent at the same time. In New Orleans, in the French Quarter, miles from the barking lungs of alligators, the air maintained this quality of breath, although here it acquired a tinge of metallic halitosis, due to fumes expelled by tourist buses, trucks delivering Dixie beer, and, on Decatur Street, a mass-transit motor coach named Desire."

—Tom Robbins, *Jitterbug Perfume*

ACROSS THE STREET from the Old Ursuline Convent sits the Beauregard–Keyes House, which was built in 1826 by Joseph LeCarpentier.

Open daily for public tours, the home displays a variety of antiques and historic bits and bobs, including some of the original furniture used by the Beauregard family. In keeping with the distinct architecture of New Orleans, the house features twin curved stone staircases, beautiful ironwork, and a brick-walled garden. The Beauregard–Keyes home is also another historic French Quarter landmark filled with haunting stories of intrigue.

The house is named after General Pierre Gustave Tou-
tant (P.G.T.) Beauregard, who was sent to Charleston, South
Carolina, during the Civil War, where he ordered his troops to
fire the first shot on Fort Sumter in 1861. Beauregard had an
illustrious career in the military, serving previously as a major
in the Mexican War. Once the Civil War was over, he returned
to New Orleans and lived in the house from 1866 until 1868.
This is where he began his civilian life, working as the president
of three railroads: the New Orleans, the Jackson, and the Great
Northern Railroad. During this time he also wrote three books
about the Civil War.

In 1904, Sicilian wine merchant Pietro Giacona purchased
the home for his family to live, though some reports say that
Pietro and his family were actually running a tax-free liquor
business from the home. The neighborhood had migrated from
its Creole roots to a popular area for Italian immigrants to reside.
The Giaconas loved to socialize and were best known for their
large, loud, and entertaining dinner parties.

On June 17, 1908, gunshots were heard coming from the
Giaconas' home, and neighbors reported hearing screams
and shouting. When the police arrived, they found three men
dead and followed a trail of blood that led from the yard over a
wall and through several streets until they caught the wounded
fourth man.

As the police investigated the murders and interviewed the
Giaconas, the Giacona family stated that they had been threatened by the Mafia. They had decided as a family that they would
not pay the extortion fees forced upon them by the La Mano
Nera ("The Black Hand"). The Mafia had established a firm
stronghold in the city by this time. Its show of strength and
domination had been clear for decades, beginning in 1890 with
the assassination of Police Chief David Hennessy to prove the
power and reach throughout New Orleans.

Lower doorway where the author saw the ghost of a young girl

Preferring to begin their negotiations with subtle communication rather than resorting to direct violence, the Mafia at the time often used a technique called The Black Hand. The intended person of interest would receive a letter stamped with a black handprint. The Black Hand letter demanded a sum of money by a certain date or else the person would suffer the consequences by losing his or her life.

The Giacona family had received one of these letters, demanding the exorbitant sum at this time of $3,000. The letter stated that if they did not pay, the entire family would be killed.

In 1908, when police arrived at the Giacona home in response to the gunshots reported by neighbors, the Giacona family shared their Black Hand letter with the police. They explained how they refused to pay the money and then prepared for the hit men to come to their home. On the night of their arrival, the Giacona family surprised them first, killing three of the four hit men. They had invited the men to their home under the ruse of having them to dinner to discuss the terms, and while the men were eating, they pulled out their guns and shot them. The police report confirmed evidence of a dinner, finding overturned plates of food and glasses of wine covered in blood splatters.

Originally, Pietro, along with his son and his nephew, were arrested for the murder of the hit men now identified as the Barraca brothers. Upon further investigation, the story was confirmed that the Barraca brothers had been there to carry out the threats that the letter had described and that the Giacona family had acted in self-defense, so the Giacona men were released. Reportedly there were several more attempts to kill the family in their home, but the Giaconas were able to protect their family by turning the home into a virtual fortress under constant guard until they moved away several years later.

In 1925, new owner Antonio Mannino reportedly wanted to tear down the home and build a macaroni factory. Neighbors and local preservationists were alarmed by the thought of the historic home being destroyed to create something industrial, so they rallied to raise the funds to purchase the home from Mannino and preserve the home as a historic property.

Beginning in 1944, Frances Parkinson Keyes rented the second floor of the home, where she resided during the winter months for the next 25 years. Frances Keyes was married to Henry Wilder Keyes, who was a former governor of New Hampshire and a US Senator. Frances was an author who wrote a column for *Good Housekeeping* and more than 51 books, including *Dinner at Antoine's*. She also enjoyed collecting items, including the 200 dolls and more than 87 teapots on display inside the home. When she died in 1970, she left the royalties of many of her books to the foundation that owns the home to help care and preserve the historic home.

Regarding the haunted history of Beauregard–Keyes, the official report has been that is not haunted. However, speak

to any tour guide or locals in the area and you'll hear numerous reports of haunting experiences. The stories are told by
locals and tourists who describe seeing a spectral apparition
or hearing unexplained noises around the home. By day the
haunting reports are quite gentle; a ghost cat circles your legs or
sometimes a ghost dog is seen scampering around the home.
The dog is believed to be Lucky, the cocker spaniel owned by
Frances Keyes.

By night the paranormal activity is reported to be down-
right sinister. A number of witnesses report seeing a full display of a Civil War battle in action, which they believe to be
a re-creation of the Battle of Shiloh. Under a full moon, the
battle begins with the roar of cannon fire. Then ghostly forms
of soldiers appear on the scene, wounded and bleeding as they
fall to the ground, writhing in pain. Horses also appear on
the battlefield scene, and the war wages on for some time. Some
have stated that along with the sights and sounds, they can also
smell smoke and other pungent smells of war.

No actual battles were ever fought here on the property, during the Civil War or otherwise, so the explanation of why this
ghostly battle scene would occur leads back to General Beauregard. While the general had some spectacular wins during the
war, the Battle of Shiloh was the most devastating loss under
his leadership. More than 3,477 men died during this battle,
with an additional staggering 2,300 men wounded. Beauregard
never fully recovered from this loss, and he spoke about his long-
suffering emotional pain and regrets about this battle.

The theories and speculations by many paranormal
researchers is that Beauregard carried this grief and guilt with
him so strongly that, as he wrote about this battle in his books,
he relived the event over and over in his mind. As he reenacted
this traumatic battle scene with his thoughts, he created an
enormous amount of psychic energy to this already volatile and

Stairway where ghosts are seen at the Beauregard–Keyes home

emotionally charged event. With the metaphysical understanding that thoughts are things and that thoughts given enough energy can create a reality, it is believed that as he wrote about the event and obsessed about it daily, he manifested a ghostly reenactment of this battle. The science of this type of paranormal event is still being studied, similar to the studies of psychokinesis and telekinesis, where objects can be moved by the mind. It still is not completely understood what metaphysical powers humans have and what can be created by the mind with the power of strong emotions attached to the thoughts. Haunted battlefields are created by the emotional pain from the actions that occur during war, which are imprinted onto the earth and reenacted with a date stamp. Objects also hold energy, both those that are directed onto the object, like a charmed ring with a spell, and those indirectly attached, such as an antique piece of furniture that absorbed the positive or negative energy expressed in a home for generations.

The theory continues to postulate that some of Beauregard's men who died in this battle attached themselves to him as ghosts. Their constant presence around him, in effect haunting him, added to his grief and continued to keep his conscious and unconscious thoughts focused on their death and the horrific battle lost.

This highly charged situation—a supernatural entanglement of his thoughts and emotional pain, creating a strong energetic field of guilt, along with the ghosts who haunted him after their death—created an energy imprint. This imprint attaches to its physical surroundings, and thus, the battle is reenacted over and over again, eventually becoming emotionally imprinted to the home where he resided at the time.

While this alone makes for a highly volatile haunted location, these are not the only ghosts reported here at the home.

Ghostly sightings of men shouting and screaming in Italian with guns firing in the courtyard and along the walkway are also reported at night. Some witnesses report seeing the men in full body apparitions and hearing gunshots, while others see shadows creeping around the bushes and in the garden. It appears that the horrific night of murder experienced by the Giacona family has also created an energy imprint here on the land.

Additional supernatural stories include people hearing the sounds of ballroom dancing and music coming from inside the home on some evenings, after the home has been closed up for the night with no one left inside. The dancing is believed by some to be General Beauregard dancing with his wife, Caroline.

During my visit to the Beauregard–Keyes home, I was fortunate to be traveling with several people who knew the home well. They agreed to speak with me as long as I promised to keep their names secret, as they said no one is allowed to speak about the ghost activity and stories.

One of these people shared that during recent renovation work on the home, contractors had discovered a doll and some old bones buried in the ground where they were digging. They were in the process of working to determine the age and date of the artifacts to determine to whom they may have belonged.

All three people shared with me that they had personally experienced ghostly sightings at the home. One of the women had felt a presence walk up to her and stay with her while she was in the home. The tour guide I had traveled with that day shared his experience of giving a late-night carriage tour past the home. He said that one evening, he and the tourists in his carriage had seen two men standing on the front porch of the home only to observe them disappearing into thin air in front of their eyes.

While standing outside the home, my psychic senses were drawn to the iron gate located below the stairs and front porch. From this area, I sensed something watching me and felt a supernatural presence in the area. As I walked closer to the gate, the entity retreated, not wishing to engage with me at this time. This was in the midafternoon, and the entity was alone and seemed rather shy. Perhaps had I been standing out there alone rather than with a group of people, the entity might have felt more comfortable communicating directly with me.

The psychic impression I had of the spirit was of a young girl. As I connected with her energy, I felt that she was attached to the old Ursuline Convent across the street. This young girl, I believe, liked to visit the home to get away from everyone at the convent. I had the feeling that she did not want to be seen out of fear of getting in trouble. She believed the nuns would not be happy to find that she was here across the street on this property. Due to her shyness and disappearing act, I was unable to determine much more about this young girl, whom I would say appeared to be somewhere between the ages of 12 and 14. I hope to hear from others who may have seen this young girl ghost during their visit to the home.

⚜ **Kala's Travel Tips**

- Ironically the original owner, **Joseph LeCarpentier,** is not memorialized in the naming of the home. LeCarpentier's grandson, Paul Morphy, is legendary in his own right as a famous chess player. Frances Keyes wrote about Paul in her 1960 book *The Chess Players*. Keyes also wrote about General Beauregard in some of her books, perhaps tapping into his spirit still lingering in the home or the energy imprints left behind. Though my research could find no proof of this, nor have I heard anyone speak about it, I have the distinct feeling that Frances Keyes had psychic ability of her own.

- Circus Square, which has always been informally referred to as **Congo Square,** had its name changed after the Civil War to Beauregard Square, though locals continued to refer to it as Congo Square. In 2011, the New Orleans City Council officially restored the name to Congo Square. Congo Square was the area where French Quarter slaves would meet on Sundays to dance, sing, play music, socialize, and set up market to sell their goods. Deep spiritual energy can be felt in this area, which was previously used by the Oumas Native American tribe for their corn feasts and was considered by the Oumas to be holy grounds. The Oumas celebrated here on this ground long before the city of New Orleans was established.

- Legends say that Joseph LeCarpentier made his living as an auctioneer and that a good portion of his inventory came from the **pirate Jean Lafitte.**

- The official stance at the home is that there are no ghosts, but many people continue to report **orbs, mists, faces, and ghost dogs** appearing in their photos taken at the home. Photographs are welcome while touring the home, so perhaps you'll capture something paranormal during your tour.

- Across the street from the home you'll see the **Old Ursuline Convent** with its windows that were once reportedly locked down with blessed screws to keep the vampires from entering. These original windows are long gone, and the new ones are hurricane proof, but you can see the area where the original windows existed.

- Paul Morphy and his family later lived in a home in the French Quarter, in what is now the location of **Brennan's Restaurant.** Paul's ghost is said to haunt both the Beauregard–Keyes home and Brennan's. In New Orleans, if you follow the history trail long enough, you'll find connections between most of the families along with their ghosts. Personally I think haunting Brennan's is a great idea, especially during Sunday brunch.

- The **Black Hand Mafia** organization in Louisiana was not to be messed with lightly. Reportedly, Al Capone took the train from Chicago down to New Orleans in 1929 to take over the bootleg operations in the city. The legend states that the Black Hand gang met Capone and his men at the train station, where they disarmed all of his men and broke all of their fingers, sending Capone and his men hightailing it back home on the next train to Chicago.

- The Beauregard–Keyes home appreciates donations to help continue the upkeep and preservation of the home. Recent damage from termites has led to considerable costs to repair and stabilize the structure of the building. While visiting, **consider making a donation** to preserve this beautiful piece of New Orleans history.

CHAPTER 19

Celebrate Jazz and Mardi Gras with the Spirits at Hotel Monteleone

"It has been said that a Scotchman has not seen the world until he has seen Edinburgh; and I think that I may say that an American has not seen the United States until he has seen Mardi-Gras in New Orleans."

—Mark Twain, *Mark Twain's Letters, 1853–1880*

THE HOTEL MONTELEONE has been the favorite haunt of many writers, including William Faulkner, Truman Capote, Tennessee Williams, Sherwood Anderson, Anne Rice, Stephen Ambrose, Ernest Hemingway, and John Grisham. Hemingway was said to have been so enchanted with the Monteleone that when he wrote *Night Before Battle*, he included the hotel as part of the setting. Tennessee Williams featured the hotel in his play *The Rose Tattoo*.

The Hotel Monteleone began with the dream of a Sicilian man named Antonio Monteleone, who was living in Italy operating a shoe factory. Monteleone heard the siren call of New Orleans from his home in Italy, and lured by the promise of opportunity and adventure, he set sail for New Orleans. Upon his arrival, Monteleone opened a cobbler shop on Royal Street.

Monteleone then purchased the hotel on the corner of Royal and Iberville Streets and began building and expanding the hotel over time, enduring the Great Depression and other economic, political, and wartime difficulties. In 1954, the original building was razed and a new foundation was laid for a new hotel to be

Entrance to the Hotel Monteleone

built on the site. The hotel is now owned by the fourth genera-
tion of the Monteleone family and continues the family tradition
dedicated to service and style.

Locals share stories about the generosity and evolutionary
progress of the hotel owners, claiming that during the stock
market crash in 1929, the hotel took care of their guests who
were in desperate straits, including forgiving their bill and going
as far as giving some now-destitute guests money to travel back
home. The hotel has always been a trendy and happenin' place,
and Liberace and Louis Prima performed at its Swan Room
nightclub, where Paul Newman was said to have visited often
when in town. The hotel lobby was the first in New Orleans to
have air-conditioning.

Generations of locals and staff from the hotel share stories
of an amazing array of paranormal activity experienced inside
the Hotel Monteleone, making it one of the most haunted hotels
in New Orleans.

Stunning view of the architectural design at the Hotel Monteleone

Many guests have reported seeing a young boy around the age of 3 running through the halls and, at times, entering their rooms on the 14th floor. Guests describe him as wearing a striped shirt. The legend surrounding this ghost boy is that he was the son of Josephine and Jacques Begere, who were guests at the hotel while visiting New Orleans.

According to the legend, sometime during the late 19th century, the Begeres traveled to the city to attend an opera at the French Opera House on Bourbon Street. Their young son, Maurice, remained at the hotel with his nanny. On their way back to the hotel after the performance, the horse pulling their carriage bolted in fear from a loud noise, causing Jacques to be thrown from the carriage, where he died on the street. Some of the legends state that during this time in his grief, Maurice contracted yellow fever and died in New Orleans, and that Josephine died within the year from a broken heart. Other stories say that Maurice did not fall ill here, but that he never recovered from the death of his father and haunts the hotel looking for his father to return back to the hotel.

Other ghost children are also reported playing on the 14th floor. It is unclear what attracts them to this particular floor, but there have been speculations that other children may have passed away at the hotel during one of the frequent yellow fever epidemics in old New Orleans. If Maurice has been at the hotel the longest, the other ghost children may have met up with him after their death. Since he prefers to roam the 14th floor, it is logical that they would play with him there.

One of the distinguishing features in the lobby of the hotel is a very large antique grandfather clock. Several people have reported seeing the shadow of a man standing by the clock, where he appears to be checking on how the clock is operating. It is surmised that it may be a former employee named William or nicknamed Red, who looked after the clock and other engineering projects at the hotel. It appears that his work did not end after he passed away, and he continues to check in and ensure that the clock is in perfect working order. Guests have also reported seeing orbs and a mist around the clock when taking photographs of the clock.

The sheer amount of haunting reports of various types may be the most distinguishing feature of this hotel. Hotel staff has long shared reports of the front door to the restaurant popping open, even after the door has been securely bolted. The doors to the café are locked each day at 2 p.m., and they remain locked for the rest of the evening. Yet on many nights, between the hours of 7 p.m. and 8 p.m., the doors will fly open, and a presence will be felt, as if someone is entering through the doors. The doors open fully and then close back together again, as if the ghost has entered the room and is shutting the doors behind him. One theory is that the mystery guest is one of the former owners from the Monteleone family, who likes to pop in and check on the progress of the hotel.

Reportedly, elevators will also open on a different floor from the number pushed, and if guests step out of the elevator to see if someone is waiting nearby, they see ghost children standing at the end of the hall, who run away giggling after being caught.

For paranormal investigators, the haunted reports are like being in a proverbial candy shop. There are reports of hearing ghost children calling for their parents, running up and down the halls, and entering rooms to open drawers and close them.

Drastic changes in temperature when spirits appear, as well as orbs and shadow people caught in photographs, have been recorded. Numerous witnesses report hearing laughter and voices with no one around, as well as seeing a ghostly young bellhop who appears to help with the luggage, only to disappear from sight.

Some of the most delightful reports are those which can only be experienced in New Orleans. These include the sights and sounds of ghostly Mardi Gras revelers appearing in the hotel in full Carnival costumes and dancing through the night. There is also a report of one ghostly guest who prefers to appear naked, wearing only a mask as he streaks through the hotel. Other guests have reported waking up in their room to see the ghost of a woman who serenades them with a series of jazz tunes. By all reports, she's quite good. If the hotel could only organize these spirits into performing at the hotel bar, imagine the show!

I once had a ghostly experience while visiting the hotel. I was in the Carousel Bar with my husband, and I promise this was before I had imbibed any cocktails. We had been touring the area and popped in to grab a quick drink. We had just placed our order, and my husband had excused himself for a moment and left the table. While sitting there alone, I began reading

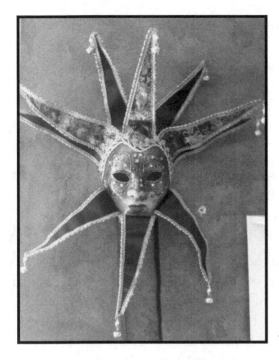

**Mardi Gras mask
from New Orleans**

some material I had brought with me. I felt my hair being touched very gently by someone standing behind me. My hair is very long, and my husband will often walk up behind me and play with my hair before putting his arm around me for a kiss. Believing it to be him in a playful and romantic mood, I turned around only to see a young girl standing there before me.

She and I looked at each other for a moment in surprise, and as I realized that she was a ghost, she giggled, putting her hand over her mouth, and then ran away. She was an adorable-looking child with ringlets of curls decorated with small bows attached to her hair, and she was dressed in a pinafore-style dress with a white-and- blue blouse underneath. Her touch was so playful and gentle, and she appeared to be a sweet child.

I look forward to returning to the Hotel Monteleone in the future and staying on the 14th floor to see more of the spectral activities. Though I have to say, given the choice, I long to see the ghostly Mardi Gras revelers and to be serenaded by the jazz singer. These events would be at the top of any paranormal enthusiasts bucket list.

 KALA'S TRAVEL TIPS

- The Vieux Carre and The Goody cocktails were both invented at the **Carousel Bar** in the Hotel Monteleone. While this author has not yet stayed at the Monteleone, she definitely has enjoyed haunting the bar there.

- Even if you've never visited the hotel in person, there's a good chance you've seen it in the movies. **The hotel has been featured in many movies,** including *Double Jeopardy* (1999) with Ashley Judd and Tommy Lee Jones, *Glory Road* (2004) with Josh Lucas and Jon Voight, *The Last Time* (2005) with Brendan Fraiser and Michael Keaton, *Retirement* (2005) with Peter Faulk, and *12 Rounds* (2008) with John Cena.

- **The hotel has also been featured on television,** including the Travel Channel segment *Weird Travels/Spirits of the South*; the HGTV episode of *Ghoulish Galas*; and the *NBC Today Show* segments "Haunted New Orleans" and "Most Famous Haunted Hotels."

- Longing to know more about Mardi Gras? Visit **Blaine Kern's Mardi Gras World,** where you can take the tour and see the artists making the floats, masks, and other decorations for Carnival each year.

CHAPTER 20

Cold Lonely Nights Lead to the Ghost of the Broken-Hearted Octoroon Mistress

"A house is never still in darkness to those who listen intently; there is a whispering in distant chambers, an unearthly hand presses the snib of the window, the latch rises. Ghosts were created when the first man woke in the night."

—J. M. Barrie, *The Little Minister*

TO COMPREHEND THE LIFE of the mistress in this story, we first must look back in history to understand what life was like during the time of slavery. In New Orleans under French rule, the laws of slavery were defined by the Code Noir, meaning "black code." This code was established by the French to control their colonial empires, including Haiti, where France had installed an enormous slave colony.

In many ways, New Orleans adopted a laissez-faire ("leave us be") attitude toward these laws, preferring to operate in their own manner as much as possible. Even though Louisiana became the 18th state in the United States in 1812, the state still operated under French-style Napoleonic law. New Orleans kept their old French customs, which differed from the rest of the United States, which operated under a puritanical British code of law regarding slavery. One such noted contrast was that New Orleans was the only city to establish an area like Congo Square, where slaves gathered to dance, play music, socialize, and sell their wares. In most other parts of America and other colonies, slaves worked on plantations,

Many stores have made this location their home. Visitors and staff often report seeing or feeling a ghost at the location.

where they toiled in the fields and then locked up each night with no outlet for expression in any manner. Americans who visited the French Quarter were often shocked and appalled that there were free people of color operating businesses and living in the city, that slaves were allowed to practice their African traditions and religion, and that French men took quadroon and octoroon mistresses. Elsewhere in America, puritanical British doctrine dictated that slaves were not allowed to embrace any of their culture or religious beliefs, nor were they allowed to live free, attend events on Sunday such as at Congo Square, or be in any type of interracial relationship as a mistress or otherwise. This led to a division of beliefs and interests as some Americans settled in New Orleans, leaving the French to keep the quarter as their part of the city and the Americans and other settlers to live west of Canal Street to uptown and the Garden District.

In the slave trade, the British, French, American, and other cultures created genetic ancestral categories for descriptions, and the laws altered according to these assigned mixed-race categories. The genetic descriptions included black, meaning both parents of black ancestry, with most coming from Africa, Haiti, and other Caribbean islands; mulatto, meaning genetically the person was half white ancestry and half black ancestry, most often the offspring of a white owner and a black slave; quadroon, which was a person with three-quarters white ancestry and one-quarter black ancestry; and octoroon, which was a person with seven-eighths white ancestry and one-eighth black ancestry.

Since there were no scientific methods of DNA testing at this time to gauge the genetic percentages, the definition assigned to a person was made from knowing their family history and lineage, or most often a judgment call based solely on how light their skin appeared. This descriptive title had strong repercussions for each person, as their resulting civil rights were based directly on how much white European blood a person reportedly had in their genetic lineage. These descriptions were recorded and determined how the person was treated culturally and socially.

The last definition was a "free person of color," which was more of a class definition, indicating that the person had bought his or her freedom or was born free, regardless of the genetic description. Some received this title from being born into a family with a quadroon or octoroon mother and white father, and others from buying their freedom from slavery or being released from slavery when the former owner passed away and gave them their freedom upon his death.

On plantations elsewhere around the country, white men took their liberties with female slaves, and from these encounters children were born, but the men never acknowledged the children, and they were described as black and slaves only. By contrast, in New Orleans wealthy white men openly courted the quadroon and octoroon free women of color, and typically, by their mid-20s, they had a relationship with one of these women as their mistress. These relationships were often established before they married a white woman a few years later and continued to exist even after their marriage.

Based on this defining nature, mulattos often had fewer privileges extended to them than quadroons, who often received fewer privileges than octoroons. Quadroon women were often groomed for the quadroon balls, where the best they could hope for in life at this time was to gain the attention of a wealthy white man at the ball, who would take them on as a mistress and provide a cottage and financial means for them and their resulting children. Octoroons fared better, as they were considered to be the most highly desired and coveted, and their families often received more money and better accommodations.

These women were considered to be some of the most beautiful women in the city with their raven hair, honey-colored complexion, and green eyes. Men in New Orleans were said to fall in love with them on first sight at the quadroon balls. There are many stories of these men professing their love to these women and wanting to marry them, but the social culture in the city and even some laws forbade this union of marriage. For example, children of these unions were not always legally considered to be rightful heirs to the family fortune, even if the man and his mistress had married.

What wasn't frowned upon legally by French Creole society was the taking of these women as mistresses. Wealthy white men would marry a white woman, many times an arranged marriage for financial, political, and business purposes to produce heirs for the family line. The husband would provide for his wife and treat her well, but in many occasions, it was a marriage of convenience with little passion. Typically the wife was also aware that her husband kept a quadroon or octoroon mistress elsewhere in the city.

On cold lonely nights, Julie can be seen shivering on the rooftop, waiting for her lover.

According to the tales, some of these men took great care of their mistresses and their children, sending their sons to private schools in Europe, where they were legally allowed to be educated. Upon their return from school, their fathers often set them up in business and left money to them after their death. Their daughters, on the other hand, were often raised to become mistresses of other wealthy white men.

Some of the French wives felt threatened by these mistresses, as many of their husbands preferred to spend more time with them than their wives. As the practice became more common, it wasn't unheard of to see a man and his wife at the Opera House sitting in a balcony, while the man's mistress was seated nearby in one of the screened box seats in back.

The men often gave their quadroon and octoroon mistresses jewelry, which were as dazzling as what the wives wore. While their dresses may not have been as extravagant, their

natural beauty often turned the heads of every man in attendance and caused a great stir. During intermission, many of
the men would excuse themselves from their wives to go spend
a few moments with their mistresses, which only angered the
wives further.

Some of the octoroon women were so light-skinned that it
was often difficult to tell their ancestral origin. This, along with
their beauty, garnered great attention as they walked through
the streets of New Orleans. In a jealous response, some of the
wives used their influence to sway the governor of Louisiana to
create a law stating that women of color could not show their
hair in public. Instead their hair must be wrapped and covered
inside a tignon, a scarf wrapped around their head.

The intention of this law was to clearly state and define a
class status, as well as to easily identify the social-class level of
a woman in public. The mistresses responded by creating beautiful tignon scarves of many colors and adorning them with jewelry and feathers. The colors in the tignon also had the effect
of highlighting their eyes and their delicately shaped facial features, often bringing more attention to their natural beauty.

It is a sad state of affairs to look at this history where the
women of this time were powerless in many ways. Most women
had few options in life and were limited to becoming a nun,
being married and dependent on a man, becoming a mistress,
or, when all else failed, becoming a prostitute. While extremely
wrong to create the law of the tignon, it is possible to see why
the wives felt so jealous and threatened.

There were so many layers to what went on during this
time in history, and each layer reveals more questions and surprises, including that some free people of color owned slaves
themselves. There are some reports—though these stories
are very rare—of men loving their mistresses so passionately
that they gave up their businesses, turned their backs on their

family and their social standing, and moved away to live in an isolated rural area to be with the women they loved.

With this understanding of how social customs and racial definitions operated in 1850s New Orleans, it's time to turn our attention to the ghost named Julie, an octoroon mistress who still haunts the city.

To tell her sad tale, first we must also understand the climate in New Orleans, which many picture as extremely hot and muggy year-round. While snow may not occur often in the Deep South, New Orleans sees its share of cold and damp winters. In fact, the humidity level creates a wet cold versus a dry cold atmosphere. Anyone who has felt the difference understands how the damp cold seeps into your body, leaving you chilled to the bone for days. During the winter months, New Orleans sees its share of cold, foggy nights and rain that can last for days.

In December of 1850, New Orleans was experiencing one of these cold winters, and people stayed inside, bundled up by the fires to keep warm and dry. On one of these winter evenings, a beautiful young woman named Julie visited her lover at his home. He had not yet married, and she was his octoroon mistress. He had provided her with a cottage, most likely off of Rampart Street where many of the mistresses lived, and since he was not yet married, she was frequently invited to visit him at his apartment on Royal Street.

By all accounts, Julie was treated well by her lover, given gifts and jewelry and treated to elaborate dinners and furnishings. While appreciative of these gifts, the one thing she desired most of all was to marry this man. While he was considered to be well-to-do, he owed all of his wealth to his family fortune, which was controlled by his father. It appears that the young man led a life of leisure and received an allowance on which he lived without having to work. He spent his days at social events and was known to entertain at his apartment with his friends well into the night. Julie would often be upstairs in his bedroom, waiting for him to come to bed after he finished drinking and playing cards with his friends downstairs each evening.

The young man knew that his father approved of him taking an octoroon mistress, but that he also demanded that the young man marry a white girl one day when a suitable arranged marriage had been found that would best serve the family interests. It was part of the bargain of living off the family fortune. Undeterred by the loss of the family money, Julie continued to press the matter of marriage on him, and they often argued about this point until it was said that he began to tire of her and the arguments. As a result, she began to be invited less often to his apartment. On one of these freezing cold December nights, Julie had been invited to visit him at his apartment, and again the conversation of marriage was mentioned. Exhausted with fighting with her, he decided to toss out an impossible demand to her, knowing that she would never go through with the ridiculous request, and thus the matter would be ended.

He told her he'd marry her if she agreed to strip naked, climb out on the roof, and stay there until the morning. As he said this, he looked out the window and saw that it was raining and close to sleeting outside. He then reportedly said, "I know it is very cold outside, but if you truly love me, your love for me will surround you and keep you warm. If you cannot complete this task, then our love is not meant to be in this way, and we will stay together as we are, with you as my mistress."

Hearing a knock on the front door, he then headed downstairs and began to drink and play cards with his friends. Other reports claim that it was just one friend at the door who visited on this evening, and that the two men drank late into the night while playing chess.

As far as Julie's lover was concerned, there was no way Julie would think of going outside in this weather, much less naked and on the roof, so he gave the matter no more thought. He entertained his friend until almost sunrise, and then headed upstairs and crawled into bed, where he planned to snuggle up against Julie and fall asleep. To his surprise, Julie was not in the bed. Looking for her around the house, he eventually went up the attic stairs and out to the roof, still not believing that he would find Julie there. To his shock and horror, she lay there on the roof, her body naked, frozen, and lifeless.

It is unclear what happened to the young man after Julie's death. Some of the reports regarding this legend say that he was in a deep state of despair over what occurred and that he dearly loved Julie and died of a broken heart a year later.

What is known is that many people who have visited or stayed in this building have reported hearing or seeing the ghost of Julie. She has been seen naked and frozen with hollow eyes staring out in pain and despair, and at other times she has been seen in a white nightgown with her arms reaching out, as if to embrace her lover.

In gentler moments, Julie has also been seen fully dressed and wandering around the home in happier times. It appears that her love for him has never ended, and she still searches the house looking for him.

Other witnesses have reported seeing the young man downstairs sitting in a chair playing chess or cards. Julie and her lover are never seen together. It's as if they are still searching for each other in the afterlife. It appears that they are both caught in moments of despair, trapped by their fateful circumstances as star-crossed lovers.

⚜ KALA'S TRAVEL TIPS

- Almost all of the **haunted tours** in New Orleans, whether walking tours or carriage rides, will bring you right up to this location, where you can see the roof that poor Julie stood on that cold December night.

- One of the most famous psychic shops in New Orleans for the past 80 years, the **Bottom of the Cup Tea Room,** used to be located in this building. When the store was in operation here, employees and customers reportedly saw the ghost of Julie. At times she appeared charming and playful and was heard giggling and roaming from the home into the garden. It seems during the month of December that her mood turns sad and she appears in her state of despair. In the spring and summer months, she enjoys the home as she once did in life.

- While visitors were having a psychic reading at the Bottom of the Cup Tea Room (when it was at this location), many often stated that Julie interacted with them during the reading. Known as one of the most reliable psychic shops in the city, **consider visiting the Bottom of the Cup Tea Room in its new location** to find out what the future holds for you.

CHAPTER 21

The Legend of St. Louis Cathedral and Pere Antoine's Alley

"Men say, that in this midnight hour
The disembodied have power
To wander as it liketh them,
By wizard oak and fairy stream . . ."
—William Motherwell, "Midnight and Moonshine"

TWENTY YEARS AFTER the Spanish assumed possession of Louisiana, Don Estevan de Miro became the governor of Louisiana in 1783. Five years later, when the Great Fire swept through New Orleans in 1788, destroying more than 90% of the buildings in the city, Miro proved himself to be a worthy governor. After the fire, Miro swung into action and reported the losses to Spain to receive financial assistance, while setting up temporary camps for survivors and opening all government warehouses to feed the people of New Orleans. He also removed all restrictions on trade and sent ships to Philadelphia to buy supplies for everyone in the city. He became one of the most popular and beloved governors of Louisiana, as residents were impressed by his compassion, organization, and efficiency.

Miro also saved the city from even more horrific tales, which no one was aware of until more than half a century later. In 1789, Miro received correspondence from a Capuchin monk, Pere Antonio de Sedella, stating that the monk was in New Orleans under secret orders from the ministry to begin the deadly Spanish Inquisition here in the New World.

Pere Antoine's Alley, where his ghost is often seen walking along the path

In these letters, Pere Sedella requested that Miro assist him in the mission by providing soldiers, which Sedella could use to round up people and begin the torturous inquisition on those who were deemed sinners and nonbelievers. Miro responded by sending soldiers to Sedella's quarters the next day. Sedella, pleased with the prompt response by Miro, thanked the soldiers but informed them that he was not quite ready to begin operations in New Orleans. The soldiers responded by following Miro's orders to place Sedella under arrest. They then hauled him to the docks, where they followed Miro's orders to put him on a ship heading to Spain. This ended the attempt to bring the inquisition and its horrors to the New World.

No one knew what Miro had done for the city, and perhaps for more cities in the New World, until 50 years later, when renovations were being done to the St. Louis Cathedral in New Orleans. During excavations, a series of underground passageways were found leading from the church to a nearby building, where secret rooms still held iron instruments of torture and other hideous items, which had been prepared for the inquisition.

Letters from Miro to Spain were also later discovered; in the letters, Miro told Spain that he was using all the creative resources he had to convince people to move to New Orleans and struggle to build a life here against the harsh conditions in the city. He reminded the Spanish officials that one of the promises to encourage people to move here to the New World had been freedom of religion. He explained that should the church begin an inquisition in New Orleans, the people would soon abandon the city and leave the goals of Spain lingering in the dust. He also stated that he would not publicly announce what Pere Sedella had come to do in New Orleans for fear that just the thought of the inquisition drawing near would instinctively cause people to flee the city.

Spain agreed with Miro, and the idea of the inquisition coming to New Orleans was terminated. Surprisingly, a few years later, Pere Sedella returned to New Orleans, this time as a Capuchin monk dedicated to serving humanity and calling himself simply Pere Antoine.

Something of a deep spiritual nature must have happened to Pere Antonio de Sedella, now known as Pere Antoine, between the time he was blocked from organizing the inquisition in New Orleans and forcibly returned to Spain by Miro to the time he returned back to the city several years later. During his second trip to New Orleans, he was a changed man dedicated to freeing the minds and liberties of his parishioners.

He served the community in New Orleans for the next 40 years, and because his secret was never revealed, he became one of the most beloved monks in the city. The reason for his popularity is that he was known to rebel against the superiors of his church and to incite his parishioners to protest against unfair practices from the government. He was known for fighting for the rights of the people, and at one point he was suspended by the church friar as a rebel rouser. When this occurred, the entire city as well as the current governor rallied to his defense and did not rest until he was reinstated to his post.

Over time he became the most beloved priest in New Orleans. On the day he died in 1829 at the age of 81, and also on the day of his funeral, every business closed and almost the entire city attended his funeral. Originally he was buried behind the St. Louis Cathedral. Later during renovations, he, along with other priests buried here, were moved to an official priest's tomb in St. Louis Cemetery. After his death, everyone began calling him a saint, as he had worked tirelessly to help the sick and dying during the epidemics in New Orleans. It was reported that he would work for weeks on end with little sleep and barely stopping to eat. Because he never became sick while caring for so many ill people, it was believed that angels protected him from illness while doing the good work.

Pere Antoine lived in a simple hut he had built on Rue Dauphine near St. Ann Street, where he had planted a date palm tree that reportedly grew very quickly and became so large that it provided shade and shelter for his simple handcrafted hut.

After his death, it is reported that hundreds of people visited his hut and literally pulled it apart piece by piece until nothing was left of the structure. Each person wanted to have a souvenir of his home, believing it to have sacred spiritual properties that could offer protection from evil and sickness. Reportedly, the entire hut was completely demolished, with every piece of it completely gone within a couple of hours. Pieces of this hut still circulate around the city through collectors and are still considered to be holy and protective. Seeds from the date palm tree were gathered by many people in the city and have been passed

Incredibly beautiful and the most famous landmark in New Orleans, the St. Louis Cathedral with a statue of Andrew Jackson in front

down through the generations. The seeds are also considered to bring great luck and spiritual protection.

Pere Antoine's beloved legacy of caring for the people of the city earned him a street name next to St. Louis Cathedral, which is called Pere Antoine's Alley. He so loved the people of New Orleans that even his death could not stop his dedication to serving the people. The legends state that his ghost is seen walking along this alley by thousands of people each year. They all describe a similar experience with the ghost. The person is walking down the alley when they see a man in a dark robe walking toward them. He never looks up, as his hands are holding a prayer book and he is deeply engrossed in reading the book. As he draws closer, it becomes apparent that he is a ghost, as people can see through parts of his robe, and he then disappears from sight. Without fail, everyone who reports this sighting also describes a deep sense of peace and comfort and feeling blessed by the experience. There has never been a report of an unpleasant encounter with Pere Antoine.

The majority of the sightings of Pere Antoine are in the early morning hours and most often during the winter months. Catholic parishioners report seeing Pere Antoine appear during Midnight Mass on Christmas Eve inside St. Louis Cathedral, where he will stand near the altar only to disappear moments later. He is also seen standing near the choir when they are singing. He is easy to spot as his Capuchin robes differ dramatically from the robes worn by the priests today. For some locals, tourists, and parishioners, when Pere Antoine appears to them in New Orleans, they are not seeing a ghost, but rather witnessing the presence of a saint.

What surprises many people to discover is that Pere Antoine and Voodoo priestess Marie Laveau had a long-lasting friendship and worked together tirelessly for decades. Pere had baptized Marie's children, and over the years, he and Marie worked together to help the sick and the poor. Marie comforted the sick and tended to hundreds of people suffering during the epidemics of yellow fever. She also counseled prisoners and worked to alleviate the suffering of poor women and children.

There is a legend that states Marie Laveau was instrumental in putting an end to the spectacle of public executions in New Orleans. During the last decade of her life, she tended to criminals on death row, helping them find peace in their final days. In 1852, she brought gumbo to Jean Adam and Anthony Delisle, two prisoners who had been accused of theft and murder. Both proclaimed their innocence, and the evidence brought against them in court was circumstantial at best. Nevertheless, the men were found guilty and sentenced to death by hanging. On the morning of their execution, Marie set up an altar in their prison cell and prayed with them. Outside the prison, more than a thousand men, women, and children gathered to watch the public execution at the gallows.

As their execution drew near, Marie provided them with a bit of alcohol, and there was also speculation that she spiced up their gumbo with herbs intended to help the men relax before they were marched to their doom.

The men continued to protest their innocence to the crowd as they were bounded with ropes and pulled up to the platform to the gallows. As they stood there on the gallows begging for mercy, the weather suddenly changed. It had been a warm sunny day with blue skies, which had encouraged the crowds to come en masse to watch the execution. As the men were led up to the platform, a breeze picked up and dark clouds rolled across the sky.

As the men pleaded for mercy, the wind began to blow. A large bolt of lightning came crashing down from the once sunny sky, hitting the ground nearby. This was followed by the sound of deafening thunder rolling in, as the skies opened with a pounding rain. The storm began to blow everything in its path around, and the branches of trees gnashed back and forth. People began to panic and run away, screaming. In the rush, the trap doors were knocked open and the two men fell below to the ground. The nooses had not yet been fully tightened around their necks, and so one of the men lay below bleeding internally and writhing in pain, while the other man's arm was twisted and broken along with his neck, which had been partially cut open from the rope. In a panic, the executioners scrambled to pull both men back up to the platform, and then hung them until they died a few minutes later.

According to the reports regarding this execution, the storm ended promptly and the formerly sunny skies returned after the two men died. The crowds rushed the platform, believing that the lightning and storm had been a message from God. In response, the policemen in attendance beat the crowds back from the platform with clubs. In the rush and panic during this event, many women and children were trampled and severely injured. The entire scene was such a display of horror that, during the next session of the legislature, a law was created which forbade any further public executions.

Marie Laveau refused to attend public executions, preferring to give comfort to the dying prisoners and praying for them inside the church upon their death. It was common knowledge that Marie had visited and cared for these men upon their imprisonment, and that she believed that they were wrongly accused. Public speculation soon spread that Marie had done her magical work and crafted a spell that gathered the elements to put on a show that day with the storm to convince the people that the men were innocent. Before the law was put into place by the legislature forbidding public executions, many residents were already swearing that they would never attend another execution and bear the wrath of queen Marie Laveau.

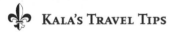 **KALA'S TRAVEL TIPS**

- Most people think of churches today as being on peaceful grounds, but St. Louis Cathedral was built next to Jackson Square, originally named Place d'Armes, where **public executions** were held. During both the French and the Spanish occupation of the city, most of the duels were fought in the center of St. Anthony's Square, located directly behind the cathedral.

- St. Louis Cathedral is the location where **Voodoo priestess Marie Laveau** prayed while holding hot peppers in her mouth to bless the peppers before putting them under the judge's chair with her magical mojo spell. The success of this court case put Marie in high regard with all the wealthy families in New Orleans.

- While it may sound odd that a Voodoo priestess would work with a priest, the principles found in Voodoo are not that dissimilar from that of the Catholic church. Over time, New Orleans–style Voodoo adopted the worship of the Virgin Mary and Catholic saints with their own gods, creating a **mixture of both spiritual cultures.**

- **Jackson Square is a paranormal researcher's delight** to spend time visiting. With St. Louis Cathedral in the middle of the square and Pirates Alley and Pere Antoine's Alley on either side, there's a good chance that you'll see or hear some ghostly activity. Measuring about 600 feet long and 16 feet wide, both alleyways were original built in the 1830s from cobblestone. Interestingly, Pirates Alley has recently become a trendy place to get married, right on the street near the Pirates Alley sign rather than inside the cathedral.

CHAPTER 22

Our Lady of Guadalupe Church and Saint Expedite

"Way down yonder in New Orleans/In the land of the dreamy scenes/There's a Garden of Eden/You know what I mean . . ."

—Louis Armstrong, "Way Down Yonder in New Orleans"

OUR LADY OF GUADALUPE CHURCH is situated in a powerful energetic area of New Orleans, located on North Rampart Street not far from where Marie Laveau once lived and adjacent from St. Louis Cemetery. The energy swirls and slides through New Orleans, moving in ribbons across the city. It's as if the muses release the energy in a new wave each month, and it ripples outward, touching various locations and people as it moves and snakes through the city.

Certain areas of the Crescent City, as New Orleans is known, are able to gather and hold these etheric forces for longer periods of time. In these locales, the energy gains strength until it bursts forth with a spirited presence, which touches the soul and brings forth inspired music and dancing. This energy can also answer the call of magic and prayers.

When this energy is trapped and allowed to stagnate, it turns dark, and the descent to madness begins to touch those caught in the pool. Magic in New Orleans begins with the awareness that the energy must be allowed to ebb and flow naturally. It cannot be forced nor contained. One must simply ride the wave when it passes by each month. Wise men and women know to mark these times and prepare accordingly to take full advantage of the energy when it comes.

The magic in this city has left its imprint on the spiritual practices. New Orleans has primarily been a Catholic-based city with a supernatural twist. The French and Spanish brought their strong Catholic base, as did the Irish in later years. This influence mixed into the proverbial spiritual gumbo, with the influx of people from the West Indies and Africa who brought Voodoo with them. Over time, the two found a way to mix well with similar devotions and prayers. Spiritual representations in both beliefs include statues, prayer altars, prayers for the dead, burning candles to the saints or gods, and rituals and masses representing body and blood. Lucky talismans for both beliefs include medals, prayer beads, palm fronds, pieces of cloth and wood, and other symbolic pieces. Voodoo practitioners were also known to create speedy results when called upon, as were saints and many of the Voodoo gods, and Catholic saints were so similar that it wasn't a far stretch to blend the two in practice.

The magic continues to spread and intermingle the ancient ways with spiritual practices. The celebration of Mardi Gras is based on the Catholic acknowledgement of Lent. The New Orleans Carnival season begins each year on January 6 at the religious celebration of the Twelfth Night (Epiphany) and continues with spectacular showstopping parades, masquerade balls, and elaborate parties until Mardi Gras, which is the French term for Fat Tuesday, signifying the day before Ash Wednesday. Ash Wednesday is a Catholic practice, which occurs 46 days before Easter. Rather than being set on a specific day, it falls on a different date each year, since Easter is based on the moon-phase calendar. Ash Wednesday is named from the Catholic practice of placing ashes on the forehead during Mass, which is a sign of mourning, and begins the season of Lent, where followers mourn the trials and death of Jesus. This practice ends on Easter Sunday.

The blessed statue of Mother Mary

Carnival is from the Latin term meaning "surrender" or "farewell to the flesh," and the season of Carnival is one of merrymaking, carousing, and having fun in general. Carnival is celebrated throughout Europe, Latin America, and the United States, most notably in New Orleans. Billed as the "greatest free show on earth," a New Orleans Mardi Gras is a sight to behold, with more than 3 million people reported to attend Carnival in New Orleans each year.

While many refer to the roots of Mardi Gras stemming from the French and Spanish Catholic traditions, history shows that Carnival began way before the religion of Catholicism. In ancient times, pagans celebrated festivals of fertility, which began in the New Year, to stir up the elemental energy around the earth to bring forth spring and renewed growth of crops, livestock, and relationships during the spring equinox.

In ancient Rome this festival was called Lupercalia, in honor of the Roman god of fertility. Many of the traditions you see in today's Carnivals are similar to this ancient tradition, including wearing costumes and masks and surrendering to the powers of Bacchus, the god of wine. Like most pagan holidays and traditions, the people refused to give them up when Christianity tried to convert them. The Roman Catholic church decided that the only way to convert the pagans was to allow them to keep their holidays and festivals and attempt to describe them in a Christian manner. Some pagan festivals were described as feasts of saints, such as the midsummer/summer solstice being referred to as St. John's Day and Halloween becoming All Souls or All Saints Day, which used to be celebrated on May 13 each year before moving it in an attempt to overtake the pagan Halloween festivals on October 31 and November 1. Lupercalia became Carnival to mark the coming of Lent, where sinners would repent. The rites, rituals, and festivals to Bacchus and other pagan gods can be seen throughout Mardi Gras each year.

As Catholicism, paganism, and Voodoo mixed in New Orleans, the saints played an important role for the groups, as people would bring offerings to the saints, pray before the statues, and light candles in their name. The mixture of these groups is where our next haunted legend begins, as Voodoo and saints mix their magic together to answer prayers and produce miracles.

The Virgin Mary is one of the most revered figures in both cultures as a representation of a Blessed Mother who cares and comforts all. The Our Lady of Guadalupe Church in New Orleans is named for the Blessed Mother, attributed to Mary as she appeared in the desert near Mexico City.

Built in 1826, the church was originally known as the Old Mortuary Chapel, where it primarily served as a burial church for victims of yellow fever. As one of the oldest churches still standing in New Orleans, it has an elaborate and eventful history, and still serves as a chapel for the police and fire departments of New Orleans today.

In the early 1800s, there were more than 23 reported epidemics of yellow fever throughout New Orleans, and the disease killed thousands of people and caused great fear and despair in the city. It was not yet understood what caused the spread of this disease, and people had all sorts of ideas, including the belief that as the dead were transported through the city to be buried, the smell coming from their bodies would permeate through the nostrils of the living and give them yellow fever. This belief was held so strongly that an ordinance was granted forbidding open-view caskets at funerals to protect the health of the living.

The Old Mortuary Chapel was built to conduct closed burials for public safety. Records show that construction of the church began on October 10, 1826, with Pere Antoine in attendance to bless the ground and the first building stone and then to place a cross where the altar would be built inside the church. The first funeral held at the church was on All Saints Day. In the early years, with yellow fever overtaking the city, no one entered the church except the pallbearers carrying the casket along with the altar boys and the priest presiding over the funeral. The grieving family and friends stood outside the church, observing the service through the open windows. At this time, no pews or seats of any kind were placed inside.

Today the Old Mortuary Chapel goes by the name Our Lady of Guadalupe Church and serves as the International Shrine of St. Jude, but locals and those in the know visit the church for a different reason: to see the magical statue of Saint Expedite.

The statue of Saint Expedite is located on the right side of the church entrance. Believers in the powers of Saint Expedite claim that he is the patron saint of quick fixes and can bring swift relief and answers to his loyal followers.

He has become the patron saint of computer programmers, engineers, and tech geeks worldwide, as prayers to him have been reported to bring swift solutions to technical problems at

The lucky statue of
Saint Expedite

hand. The pilgrimage to see this saint has only increased in recent years, as he is also said to help those out of work find employment. Many loyal followers in the tech industry report-edly swear that by placing his photo on or near their computers while asking Saint Expedite for things to work smoothly and efficiently, their problems are quickly resolved. He is also said to bring assistance to store owners, sailors, and those involved in lawsuits. He also provides encouragement to those desiring to no longer procrastinate.

The history of Saint Expedite begins with a local legend. The nuns at Our Lady of Guadalupe Church were opening crates full of Catholic statues that had been delivered to the church. One of the crates had no name listed for the statue, and the only informa-tion written on the crate was the word *expedite,* which means to deliver quickly. The legend states that the nuns, having no idea who this statue was, named him Saint Expedite after reading it on the crate. This story has been passed down in New Orleans for so many years that most people believe the story to be true.

As a good French (Scottish, Irish, and German) woman and author committed to uncovering all myths, historic stories, and legends to the best of my ability, I must exclaim, "Au contraire mon frère." I must correct this story and proclaim that Saint Expedite was not named after a stamp on his crate; rather, he is a true saint in the Catholic church bearing this name.

Saint Expedite began his life as a Roman soldier and had been known to perform miracles in cities throughout Europe long before his arrival in New Orleans. His statue is often depicted with him stepping on top of a crow while holding a cross inscribed with the word *hodie*. The crow is a symbol of tomorrow, due to the sound he makes, "caw, caw," which sounds like the Latin word *cras*, which means "tomorrow."

Expedite is holding the crow underfoot, symbolizing to do what is possible today rather than to put it off until tomorrow. The word *hodie* is a German term that means "today," again symbolizing to take action immediately. The worship of Saint Expedite, or Saint Expeditus, depending up which part of the world he is revered, was said to have begun in the Middle Ages in Turin.

So many people have received swift relief after praying to Saint Expedite that he has received something of a cultlike following. Voodoo practitioners in New Orleans associate him with the spirit of Lakwa, connected with cemeteries and Samedi, the spirit who is associated with quickly curing diseases for those who it is not their time to die. Followers of both religions swear by his miracles, and there appears to be yet another resurgence of interest in his abilities.

Perhaps you'll visit the Our Lady of Guadalupe Church during your next trip to New Orleans to see the statue of Saint Expedite in person. Until you are able to do so, the photo here in this chapter was taken directly at the church during my last visit to New Orleans. You may be able to tap into the energy here by leaving the book open to this page, where you can touch the photo and send your prayers directly to Saint Expedite when needed. If you are reading this book as an e-book, pull up the photo of Saint Expedite and ask him to intercede on your behalf, especially if it is of a technical nature.

 KALA'S TRAVEL TIPS

- It is said that **offerings to the saints,** just like the Voodoo gods, are expected when asking for a favor or wish to be granted. Locals claim that Saint Expedite prefers wine, rum, and sweet cakes, with a special penchant for pound cake. Offerings are not allowed at the chapel, so many people slip a small piece of paper with their prayer under the statue and then visit the gravesite of Marie Laveau with their offering, asking her to deliver it to Saint Expedite.

- When visiting Saint Expedite in New Orleans, I connected with his energy and a prayer to him formed on my lips as I mingled with his spirit. **If you would like to ask Saint Expedite for a favor to be granted,** consider printing out his photo and placing it on your altar while lighting a red candle and saying this prayer that was given to me:

> *"Oh Mighty Saint Expedite,*
> *Bring Swift Relief to My Problem At Hand."*

Then explain your situation and problem. Say the prayer three times and don't forget to offer a piece of cake and rum in offering. The luckiest day of the week to say this prayer is Wednesday, which is associated with the planet Mercury, the

messenger, and on his Feast Day, which is April 19. Many
practitioners state that once Saint Expedite answers your
prayer, it is very important that you do a good deed or make a
donation in his name.

- During my visit to the church, I found it to be full of spirits,
  which is not surprising given how many funerals were performed here through the years and given the location near the
  cemeteries. Even with the overwhelming amount of spiritual
  activity, the energy here is actually relaxing and peaceful. People visit daily to slip small papers under Saint Expedite and
  make their requests. If you decide to do this, **please consider
  making a donation to the church,** for they have to look after
  his statue and care for the surroundings, making it possible
  for you to visit. Saint Expedite is perhaps the most photographed statue of any saint in the city, as many believe that
  his photograph helps one intercede directly to him in prayer.

CHAPTER 23

The Resident Ghosts of Yesteryears and Pat O'Brien's

"The painting that I painted is a spell to revitalize New Orleans, since New Orleans is home to mysticism and voodoo in the United States."

—Danny Simmons

CONTINUING OUR JOURNEY through the spirit and spirits of New Orleans, the city showcases the diverse cultures. The fascinating history of the Creole and Cajun cultures are portrayed in the music and cuisine, the Spanish and French architecture are apparent throughout the city, and the soulful influence of the Caribbean and African people provide the pulse and vibe of the Crescent City.

The most unique combination of ingredients blend together to make the best gumbo; the same can be said about creating a city. Each culture that settles in a region indelibly leaves its mark and impact on the area. In New Orleans history, this includes the cultures listed above along with the migration of the Irish.

Between the 1820s and 1840s, a great potato famine hit Ireland. During this time, Irish farmers were forced to export wheat, barley, and oats to Britain, forcing the Irish to eat the only crop left—the potato. A fungus attacked the potatoes, causing them to rot, and the Irish people began to starve. The magnitude of this famine—along with the politics of the time with England, which did little to help the Irish with this plight—caused almost 1 million Irish to die from starvation and malnutrition. It also encouraged almost 1 million Irish people to migrate to

Pat O'Brien's serves up hurricane cocktails and fun!

the New World. Britain reportedly refused to help the starving
Irish, saying that the money would be used to purchase guns to
fight for their independence against Britain. At one point during the influx of the Irish to America, there were as many Irish
arriving in the port of New Orleans as in New York.

When looking at American history, it can be said that Ireland's
loss was America's gain, as the country benefited in a myriad of
ways from the Irish settling here in the United States. At first
their arrival was a bit rocky, as most of the immigrants suffered
from malnutrition and carried diseases that began to spread in the
American cities as they arrived. This led to them being shunned
by parts of society in the port cities, which had already been deal-
ing with a number of epidemics for decades. The Irish spirit pre-
vailed, and as they settled into their new homes and their health
returned, they established themselves in the New World. Their
influence is a large part of Americana that we see today through
cultural celebrations, including Halloween and St. Patrick's Day.

The Irish who immigrated through the port of New Orleans settled in an area near the river later named the Irish Channel. The culture in New Orleans welcomed them, as the French and Spanish settlers were also anti-British on most accounts. The Irish took many of the worst jobs in the city in order to survive. At great peril and with a tremendous loss of life due to disease, snakes, and alligators, the Irish were instrumental in digging and establishing the New Basin Canal, an extensive shipping canal system that provided an important link from New Orleans to Lake Pontchartrain. Building the New Basin Canal was extremely difficult; the Irish worked in water up to their hips while digging and were constantly at risk of contracting malaria, cholera, and yellow fever, all of which were fatal to most. Many of the Irish laborers who fell ill while working were buried at or near this area, with some estimates claiming that the number buried could be 10,000 and others saying it could be as high as 30,000. As just one example, a cholera epidemic at this time killed more than 6,000 people in three weeks. So many people died during these epidemics that the numbers are staggering.

The Irish added to the diversity of architecture and culture in the city, building St. Patrick's Catholic Church and establishing Hibernia Bank. One example of Irish architecture is the Gallier House on Royal Street, built by Irishmen James Gallier and his son James Jr., who were architects in the city. Another testament to the strength and heart of the Irish is the statue of Margaret Haughery, an Irish immigrant who became a well-respected businesswoman in New Orleans. Both of her parents died in her youth, and her husband died in his 20s, quickly followed by the death of her child. Alone in the world, Margaret worked her way up from working in a bakery to owning the bakery. Her business acumen was only matched by her good deeds and charity, and the statue portrays her comforting an orphan in her arms. She was known as the "bread woman" throughout the city, always feeding the poor from her bakery and helping widows and orphans however she could, including building several orphanages. When she died, she left all of her wealth to charities in the city, with the stipulation that assistance would be granted to all widows, orphans, and the elderly in need, regardless of their religion. It is believed that this statue of Margaret is the first statue in the United States to honor a woman.

While the Irish experienced some dark days during the famine and the rebuilding of their lives in the United States, they also carried with them a tremendous spirit of hope, survival, and love of life. The first St. Patrick's Day celebration was held in New Orleans in 1809, and an Irish theater was established soon after. They also brought their own brand of Celtic magic and lore with them, which eagerly intermingled with the brewing and brooding magical energy running through the city.

The most famous location to tap into the spirit of the Irish while visiting New Orleans is Pat O'Brien's. With its signature flame fountains (water fountains with fire in the middle) in the courtyard, live music, and drinks served up in souvenir glasses, Pat O'Brien's delivers on its motto created in 1933, which is simply, "Have fun!"

Located in the heart of the French Quarter, Pat O'Brien's has an illustrious history, first as a speakeasy during Prohibition and then operating as an Irish bar. Perhaps what it's most famous for is serving its popular drink, the hurricane, in a beautiful glass shaped like a hurricane lamp, which you can take home with you after you finish your drink in the bar. Almost every visitor to New Orleans has a Pat O'Brien's hurricane glass back home as a souvenir of their good times in the city.

I usually end up at Pat O'Brien's at one point or another during every visit to New Orleans, and the last time was to watch the Saints game. It was during this trip to Pat O'Brien's that I saw my first ghost there, though I had previously visited

The famous fire
and water fountains
in the courtyard at
Pat O'Brien's

many times and never encountered any paranormal activity. I was in the bar chatting with some locals wearing Saints jerseys. Also in the bar was a large group of New York Giants fans fueling up for the big game that evening. They were pretty funny, and everyone was having a good time laughing and joking around about the game.

Most of these guys were really fun, but as the afternoon went on, two of them had become really drunk and were pretty nasty in what they were now saying. They were even yelling at and personally insulting Saints fans through the window as people walked by or entered the bar. These unsuspecting people, who were simply walking by outside, were startled as the men yelled and cursed at them.

Disturbed by their aggressive actions, I declared in the bar that I was putting the mojo on the game. I said that the Saints would win the game that night, and not only would they win, but that we would also provide such a spanking that these Giants fans would return home shamed.

I wiggled my hands, shook a little Tabasco on the table, and declared the magic mojo to be so! As fortune would have it, it was a chilly November day in New Orleans and I was wearing a long black cape. As I stood up to go to the ladies' room, the breeze blew around me, lifting my cape and giving credence to the words I had just uttered. These men looked at me and at each other, wondering if perhaps the Voodoo stories they heard about New Orleans and Saints fans were true.

I dashed off to the ladies' room, still grumbling about what some of the men had said to fans walking by on the street. As I came out of the stall and bent over the sink to wash my hands, I noticed a person standing at the sink next to me and said, "Can you believe what those men were saying about Saints fans? They'll eat their words later tonight." The person standing next to me at the sink replied, "Yes, ma'am, they will indeed," which caught me off guard as it was a man's voice. As I looked up, an elderly African-American gentleman was standing there next to me. He was wearing black pants, a white shirt, and a black vest, which was unbuttoned. He had a small towel in his hands, which he reached out to me. As I extended my hand toward it, my hand went straight through the towel and his hand. Ironically, what shocked me first was that he was a man in the ladies' bathroom, rather than the fact that he was a ghost.

He was very sweet, and though he held nothing in his hands but a towel, I got the distinct impression that he had been a musician and perhaps had played at Pat O'Brien's in the courtyard in previous years. He cheered me up immensely, and I returned back to the bar more certain than ever that the Saints would indeed win the game that night with the confirmation from the spirit world. I can happily report that the partying, shouting, and carousing that happened later that night throughout the city was the celebration of the Saints winning the game with a whopping 49 points over the Giants 24.

I hope to see this ghost again next time I return to Pat O'Brien's, as he was such a sweet gentleman. He was so cognizant of what was going on in modern day, as he had followed my conversation and knew exactly what I was talking about with the game. I also feel that he's a lucky sign, and if you see him, your wish will be fulfilled. It's a bit shocking at first to see him in the ladies' restroom, but he's so sweet that you'll quickly move past the initial surprise.

Whenever I visit New Orleans, my magical energy always stirs and my muse awakens. Throughout my life, I've have had at least three dreams each night that I remember each morning upon awakening. In New Orleans, these dreams are always more vivid with my psychic sensitivities at full charge. I've shared my dream about the French Opera House in chapter ten, and now I'll share the second dream I had while in the city.

One night in New Orleans I dreamed about a store that I should visit while in the French Quarter. I saw myself inside the store walking around and looking at a variety of metaphysical items, along with having a chat with a very contented-looking cat watching over the store. In my dream he said to me, "This is my store. Come visit me." He had the perfect New Orleans accent, which newcomers might assume sounds like the deep Southern drawl, but it's more of a mix of a Southern accent blended with a Brooklyn accent. Like everything delicious in New Orleans, it's the mix of cultures that creates this unique style.

Right before I awoke from the dream, I heard someone whisper in my dream and say, "It's Yesteryears." I wasn't sure what this meant when I woke up. Was this a store that had once existed in New Orleans and was long gone in the past? Could the voice be referring to a past life, a yesteryear, when I had visited this store? I couldn't quite make peace with this analogy, as in the dream I looked like myself today rather than from a past life.

I asked the concierge at my hotel about it, and he replied that he was not familiar with a store by that name. Not having time to research further, I headed out that morning to go meet with some people with whom I had an appointment to discuss the history of New Orleans. While walking through the French Quarter on the way to my appointment, I sent a message to the universe and said, "I remember the dream, and if there's something for me there with yesteryear, I need your guidance to show me what to do." With my message sent out through the spiritual airwaves, I arrived at my appointment and my day began to fly by quickly.

By late afternoon, I had wrapped things up, and while walking back from Jackson Square, my husband and I decided to stop into Pat O'Brien's and grab a bite to eat before going back to the hotel. There are two entrances to Pat O'Brien's, one from St. Peter Street and the other from Bourbon Street. For some reason, I always tend to enter from the St. Peter's entrance, probably to avoid the crowds on Bourbon Street.

On this occasion, for the first time, I entered from Bourbon Street, and when I left, I exited from Bourbon Street into the crowd. As I paused there in the street to decide which direction to take, I caught a pebble in my shoe. Leaning on my husband while standing in the street, which is more common than you would think on Bourbon Street, I took my shoe off to shake out the pebble. While doing so, I looked up to see the sign of a store in front of me that read Yesteryears!

I was so excited that I was hopping around with my shoe in hand and trying to explain to my husband what I was seeing while he was counseling me to put my shoe back on before I took off running. With my shoe firmly back in place, we left the street and climbed the stairs to enter into the shop.

As I first entered, I marveled at how everything in the store looked just as it had in my dream, and as I walked toward the

Yesteryears—did the author find it or did it find her through her dreams? Also shown is the upstairs balcony where ghost girl is seen.

back of the store, I saw pet food and water dishes and knew that the cat from my dream must be nearby.

Within seconds, the cat appeared and made his presence known that he indeed was the caretaker of the store. Knowing that I was meant to visit the store, I walked around to see what would happen next. The owner struck up a conversation with me, and we ended up having a lovely chat about the city. She introduced me to another man in the store who was a local historical guide. The three of us had a wonderful conversation about some of the places I had just visited while researching the book.

Front window where the author's pendant was waiting for her inside

At the same time, I was looking around the store for a pendant that I had seen in my dream, which looked very much like it carried what I call mermaid energy. I looked all throughout the store, but to my disappointment I could not see the pendant anywhere. I was just about ready to give up and leave when my psychic senses said to stay a while longer.

I sat down for a moment to chat further with the owner, and the cat came walking beside me again. The owner asked me if she could help me with what I was looking for, and I replied that I had been looking for a pendant, but that I had searched all of her cabinets and the one I was looking for was not there.

The cat had been near me during this conversation, and to my amusement, when I said I could not find the pendant, he hopped up on a nearby table where several necklaces were lying in jewelry boxes. He began to put his paws in the boxes and pulled out the necklaces and the lining inside the boxes. The shop owner was not too pleased with his actions, but I was greatly amused and saw it as a communication from him to dig deeper to find what I was searching for.

I said to the owner, "I thought that the pendant I was seeking was here, and I've searched the cabinets. Is there anywhere else I should look?" She thought for a moment, and then I saw her face light up as she said, "There are some that I've had for many years and have not pulled them out in a very long time." She went around by the front window of the shop and pulled two pendants out and brought them to the counter. As soon as I saw the green pendant, I recognized it immediately from my dream and knew I had to have it. I was so excited that I said, "I'll take it," realizing a moment later that I hadn't even looked at the price. She kindly wrapped it up for me, and later that evening back in the hotel, I wore the pendant so that stones and I could begin to connect energetically, which happened almost immediately.

On a recent trip in North Carolina, I was wearing the pendant and had one of the strongest psychic connections regarding water that I have ever experienced. This particular pendant is completely connected to the element of water and holds a unique variety of qualities that I am still working on to fully understand and comprehend.

While this experience was incredible on its own, I also had the opportunity to hear from the store owner about the ghost who haunts Yesteryears and lives on the second floor of the shop. The second story of the shop is rented out as an apartment, and tenants often hear the ghost of a young girl walking around. She is often seen with auburn hair and wearing a lace dress. When she appears, she is fond of playing with the dolls, masks, and wind chimes in the store. The general consensus is that the ghost drifts between the apartment above the shop and down into the store to check things out. I imagine that she and the cat caretaker have a good time together.

I dearly enjoyed my time at Yesteryears. In the back is a room for psychic and tarot card readings. I felt so at home here that I wondered if perhaps I had spent some time in this building in a past life. It felt so warm and welcoming and completely comfortable that though I physically walked into this shop for the first time, I knew the layout from my dream.

Next time I'm in New Orleans, I'd love to spend a few days offering readings in the shop, if the owner and the cat caretaker would have me, as the energy there is so conducive for psychic readings as well as discovering unique magical treasures waiting to come home with you.

Magic mojo and the luck of the Irish may have been with me on this trip, as the Saints won their game, and I found the pendant from my dream, both within steps of each other at Pat O'Brien's and Yesteryears.

While reading this, here's my wish for you: May the luck of the Irish be yours while you enjoy the food, music, shopping, and festivities in New Orleans!

⚜ KALA'S TRAVEL TIPS

- Visit the historic **Gallier House,** now a local museum located on Royal Street.
- At Pat O'Brien's enjoy a signature **hurricane drink** in a souvenir take-home hurricane glass.
- Order your very own **Pat O'Brien's Mardi Gras beads** to wear at your next St. Patty's Day party.
- There's no **St. Patrick's Day parade** quite like the one in New Orleans, where cabbages, potatoes, and other produce are tossed from the floats.
- Across the street from Pat O'Brien's is **Reverend Zombie's House of Voodoo,** which is a great place to visit. I once had a reading here in 2004 that was spot on. Some psychics left the area after Katrina and have not returned, while new ones have now moved to the area to support the city.

- You don't have to dream about your pendant to find something magical and delightful at **Yesteryears;** just visit the shop and let the magic reveal the gift for you. Don't hesitate to ask the wise cat who appears ready to assist you in the shop.

- Established in 1822, the **Girod Street Cemetery** was an above-ground cemetery with more than 2,000 wall vaults and 1,000 tombs, with some tombs rising eight tiers high above the ground. Over the decades 30,000 people were buried here. Over time, the privately owned cemetery languished in great disrepair and was all but forgotten. In 1957, the cemetery was deconsecrated, and the remains were moved to other cemeteries. Workers moved in with bulldozers, and to their surprise, the unsightly excavation of human bones and remains were pulled up with each dig of the shovel, proving that not all of the bodies had been identified and moved to a new location.

  On these burial grounds, the **Louisiana Superdome** was built, which is the home to the NFL's New Orleans Saints. Legend has it that the spirits were angry and restless after being moved from their burial grounds, so they cursed the Saints from winning. To counteract this curse, Voodoo priestesses were routinely called in before football games to appease the spirits and ask for their forgiveness. Catholic priests and nuns also attend the games to bless the stadium, while sprinkling holy water and calling in Saint Michael to assist the spirits in letting go and moving on.

  Reportedly, after Hurricane Katrina in 2005, so many residents sought shelter from the floodwaters inside the Superdome that the curse was lifted by the spirits, who felt so sorry for the people of New Orleans and the enormous price they paid during the flood. These spirits now comfort the people of New Orleans and support their home team, opening the pathway for the Saints to win their first-ever Super Bowl on February 7, 2010.

CHAPTER 24

The Ghost Children of the Andrew Jackson Hotel

"Leaving New Orleans also frightened me considerably. Outside of the city limits the heart of darkness, the true wasteland begins."

—John Kennedy Toole, *A Confederacy of Dunces*

LOCATED NEAR THE CORNSTALK HOTEL on Royal Street, the Andrew Jackson Hotel sits on the former location of the U.S. District Court in Louisiana. Here in 1815, General Andrew Jackson was held in contempt of court for refusing to lift martial law in the city until he had received confirmation that the British had fully retreated and were no longer a threat to New Orleans.

From what I can discern from old court records, Jackson ordered the arrest of a Mr. Louis Louallier, believing him to be delivering information to the British during the Battle of New Orleans. Judge Hall was asked to sign the order of arrest, which he refused to do based on a lack of evidence. In response, under the power given to him during martial law, General Jackson placed both Judge Hall and Mr. Louallier in jail.

A writ of habeas corpus was presented to the court, demanding that Louallier be released. A writ of habeas corpus is a court order that demands that the prisoner be taken immediately to the court and that the court must determine if there is enough evidence to continue to hold the person in jail.

As the clerk was attempting to deliver the writ to the judge, Jackson reportedly wrested it out of his hand to stop it from

The Andrew Jackson Hotel

reaching the judge. He declared that he would not allow this prisoner to be freed until it was confirmed that the British had fully retreated and that peace was established, as he believed Louallier to be a danger if set free. The judge indicted Jackson and charged him with obstruction of justice, citing that Jackson had no authority to place an order on who could be arrested or held in jail.

It's difficult to imagine Jackson being treated in this manner after returning to New Orleans as a war hero and significantly contributing to the defeat of the British by sending them packing out of Louisiana. However, when we consider that Jackson had also engaged in more questionable activities, including recruiting pirates such as Jean Lafitte to help in the battle, it becomes easier to see that he may have had his fans and his enemies in the city. While the French residents applauded his efforts, including recruiting Lafitte, the Americans were not as pleased with his methods.

When brought into court, Jackson refused to speak about the matter, was fined $1,000, and was released. It appears that he did not pay the fine, as Congress later ordered him to pay the fine with interest, which by then amounted to more than $2,700. Given that Jackson later became president of the United States despite this conduct, it's interesting to see how times have changed. Should a presidential candidate act in such a manner today, it is unlikely that he would be elected to office.

The original building at this location was demolished in 1888. The new building constructed at that time still stands today, now operating as a hotel. The hotel receives occasional reports from guests who claim to see the ghost of Andrew Jackson in the halls, stomping his feet and shaking his hands in anger.

While Jackson's ghost roaming the halls is fascinating enough for any historian and paranormal researcher, other ghosts are reported in the building as well. The majority of ghostly reports date back to the time when the building was used as a boys' public school. During one of the frequent epidemics of yellow fever in New Orleans, the local lore says that several of the boys who attended the school succumbed to the illness and died. Other stories say a minor fire broke out in the building, and some of the boys died by smoke inhalation during the fire. The legend states that the ghost boys are seen inside the hotel and playing on the grounds. Witnesses report hearing children laughing, calling out names, and feet stomping and running up and down stairs, as well as playful shouts and squeals coming from the courtyard late at night when no one is around.

During a visit to New Orleans, I stopped by to see the Andrew Jackson Hotel. I had heard haunted stories about the place from dozens of people, so I was excited to check it out. I was not a guest of the hotel, so I did not experience staying overnight on the second floor, where many ghost sightings are reported in the evening.

I did walk the grounds right next to the Cornstalk Hotel, where I spent some time as well.

Many times when I visit a haunted site, especially one reported to be full of children, the ghost children are quick to approach and communicate with me. While here on the grounds, I did not observe any ghost children on this day. I can't say that the hotel isn't haunted, for there are reports by people who have had ghost experiences in their rooms or in the halls in the evenings. I didn't stay at the hotel, so I can only report my experience and opinion of what was occurring here on this property.

Based on my psychic feeling, I feel that the type of haunted activity occurring in the hotel may be more of a time-loop haunting, a different type of paranormal occurrence.

In a time-loop haunting, an incident that has a very strong emotional impact occurs on a property. A negative experience or sudden, tragic death leaves an energy imprint on the property that is then played over and over, like a recording of the incident that continues to loop and replay.

For example, if a fire did burn inside this building and some perished from the fire, the energetic recording of this incident could still exist, and guests would see the boys and hear running and shouts. Additionally, it's easily understandable that since the building also existed as a courthouse, there was a great deal of emotional trauma as people were sentenced of crimes, as well as the angry outrage by Jackson, who had risked his life to save New Orleans only to defend his actions here in the court. While this type of incident did not involve a death, the outburst of energy could create a historic time-loop recording that is imprinted and seen again and again, such as Jackson storming down the hall.

While I don't have access to the records of when witnesses most report seeing Jackson, I would love to be able to gather this data and see if more reports occur during the month when Jackson was indicted here on the property.

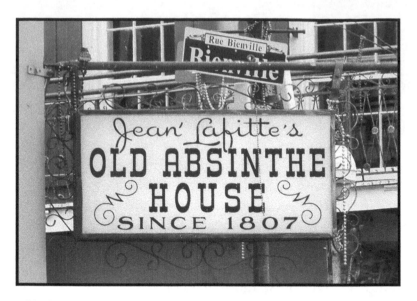

Old Absinthe House, where legends say Jackson and Lafitte once met
to discuss plans

These types of paranormal time-loop imprints happen
more often than people are aware. Famous examples include
battlefields such as Gettysburg from the Civil War, but many
private homes where great arguments transpired or other traumatic or highly emotional experiences occurred also hold this
type of energy. The Beauregard–Keyes home may be another
example of this type of time-loop haunting.

My feeling is that this is the type of paranormal activity that
guests of the Andrew Jackson Hotel are reporting. The difference with this type of haunted activity is that the ghosts are
time-loop energetic recordings, rather than ghosts who actively
haunt the site and interact with people in modern times. This
would explain why I was unable to connect with the ghost boys
while visiting the property.

During my research and investigation, I also found that
the stories reported by witnesses who stayed at the hotel over

the years were very similar, with only slight differences in details. For as many stories as I heard about children running day and night, I would expect to hear new accounts with different details of sightings and interactions if the children were actively engaged with the guests in modern time.

I feel that a haunting of this type is important to cover, as it explains how a time-loop imprint can create paranormal activity in a building and remain on the land even when a new building is built over the old one. I once lived in a haunted house with a time-loop impression. Many times I would watch the ghost of a man walk upstairs in this home, in an area where stairs did not exist in the newly constructed home where I lived. When seeing a ghost of this type, they do not interact with anyone, for they truly are not there. All that is left is the impression of the event in its recorded form.

In this case here at the hotel, it would be nicer to know that the boys who did lose their lives, whether due to the fire or an epidemic, have moved on to the other side and are at peace rather than still active here as ghosts.

⚜ KALA'S TRAVEL TIPS

- Almost all of the haunted **ghost tours** in the city will take you on a walking tour or carriage ride, where you can visit the Andrew Jackson Hotel and the Cornstalk Hotel in the French Quarter.

- Visit the **Louisiana State Museum** near Jackson Square to see an incredible variety of historical items on display, including information regarding the Battle of New Orleans and Andrew Jackson.

- One of the most famous **statues** in New Orleans is that of Andrew Jackson on his horse, located in Jackson Square in front of St. Louis Cathedral.

CHAPTER 25

The History and Mystery of the Baroness and Her Pontalba Apartments

"And you find as a writer there are certain spots on the planet where you write better than others, and I believe in that. And this [New Orleans] is one of them."

—Jimmy Buffett

UPON THE DEATH OF HER FATHER in 1798, when she was only 3 years old, the Baroness de Pontalba, Micaela Leonarda Antonia Almonester, became one of the wealthiest women in New Orleans. Her father, Don Andres Almonaster y Rojas, had been a very generous benefactor in New Orleans, providing the funds to build the St. Louis Cathedral. After the Great Fire of New Orleans, Don Andres was instrumental in the rebuilding of the city. His projects included the Cabildo, a chapel for the Ursuline nuns, two hospitals, and a boys' school. Upon his death, he was buried at St. Louis Cathedral, where his spirit could rest surrounded by what he had lovingly built in the city.

In 1811, at the age of 15, Micaela was forced by her mother, Louise, to marry her French cousin, Xavier Celestin Delfau de Pontalba, and moved to France to live at his family estate. Louise had received a letter from Celestin's father, Baron Pontalba, stating the benefits of combining the family fortunes to strengthen both sides.

Louise still controlled Micaela's inheritance, and the rumors stated that the mother was eager to send her daughter away to

Balconies of Pontalba Apartments, which provide views of Jackson Square

Europe. The arranged marriage orchestrated by the baron was his attempt to gain control of Micaela's substantial fortune. Unbeknownst to Louise, the Pontalbas had their European title and family estate, but financially they were in dire straits.

Micaela was in love with a young man in New Orleans, whom was deemed by her mother to be unworthy of marriage due to his poor economic status. Once Louise received the proposal of an arranged marriage with Micaela's cousin, Louise quickly informed Micaela that she would not be allowed to marry the young man in New Orleans. Instead, she was forced to marry her cousin after only a three-week engagement. Neither Micaela nor Celestin wanted to be married to the other. The resulting marriage was cold and loveless, and Micaela later shared that her in-laws held her prisoner in France at their estate.

The purpose of the marriage on the groom's side was to gain control over Micaela's sizable fortune. What they didn't know at the time was that Louise never had any intention of handing over

Side street view of the Pontalba Apartments

Micaela's inheritance to the Pontalbas. Throughout Micaela's life, Louise had always stirred controversy in New Orleans. When she married Micaela's father, she was 30 years younger than Don Andres. When he died, she quickly remarried a man much younger than she was, reportedly around the age of 25. Her lack of grief and mourning over the passing of her husband, as well as her quick remarriage, sparked outrage in New Orleans, as Don Andres was beloved and mourned by the community. The Creole community acted out over this disrespect to her deceased husband by creating a charivari, a social custom where people gather to publicly embarrass the person who has done a great moral wrong, such as adulterers and abusers.

During a charivari, a crowd gathers around the person's home, making loud noises and staging mock reenactments of the shameful act. A large group of people in the city staged a charivari against Louise for her lack of mourning for her husband before remarrying a much younger man. Reportedly,

Louise had to pay the crowd off with thousands of dollars before they would depart and leave her in peace. It appears that Louise was wrapped up in her life, and when the offer of marriage came through for Micaela, she was happy to ship her away while holding on to all of her money.

Back in France, it soon became clear to Micaela's father-in-law that he would not gain control over her inheritance. In 1834, now a full adult and mother, Micaela sought a divorce from her husband. In a last attempt to gain control of her inheritance before she could obtain a divorce, Micaela's father-in-law shot her four times with a pair of dueling pistols and then committed suicide. Against all odds after being shot at close range, Micaela survived. She was left with permanent damage, including her a disfigured left breast that was left heavily scarred and two mutilated fingers, which occurred as she attempted to deflect the bullets from her body. Upon the death of her father-in-law, her husband became the baron, giving Micaela the title of baroness. Eventually she was able to separate and escape from her husband and return to New Orleans.

Described as a flamboyant redhead who physically resembled her father, the baroness returned to her beloved city. With her incredible wealth restored to her, she became a real estate mogul in New Orleans, who designed and built the Pontalba Buildings in the French Quarter. In the beautiful ironwork in the balconies surrounding the buildings, she had her initials and her father's initials monogrammed in the railing. In creating these striking buildings and surrounding gardens, she helped preserve the oldest and most historic area in New Orleans. In doing so, she also created one of the best locations in the city to see the ghosts who still call this area home.

The Pontalba Apartments are some of the oldest apartment buildings in the United States. Built in the 1850s by the baroness as row houses, they are located on both sides of Jackson

Square. Micaela's dedication to building these dwellings also included renovating the area around St. Louis Cathedral and the square to make them more attractive and appear like the beautiful squares in Europe. For this design, she had the landscaping laid out in a sunburst pattern with the pathways extending out like the rays of the sun. Reportedly, the cost of this project at the time was more than $300,000 and took almost three years to complete.

In the buildings today, the ground floors have been converted into stores and restaurants, and the upper three floors are apartments. Based on the real estate concept of "location, location, location," it's difficult to top the magnificent location of the Pontalba Apartments. The balconies offer views of the Mississippi River along with Jackson Square. Right outside the apartments is Café du Monde and the French Market, and only steps away are the best restaurants, clubs, and shops in town.

The Pontalba Apartment balconies provide a bird's-eye view for people watching from above, as the surrounding area is continuously filled with tourists, artists, musicians, carriage tour drivers, and shopkeepers going about their days. It's also known as one of the best locations to see ghosts running through Pirates Alley, Pere Antoine's Alley, down the streets to the river, alongside Jackson Square and the Cabildo, and around St. Louis Cathedral. The ghost stories here are not focused on inside the apartment building, but rather around the physical landmark location.

Many of the stories shared in this book can trace their steps to Jackson Square. It is said that ghost pirates, as well as the haunted spirits of those who were publicly executed in the square, still roam the streets. Many prisoners died while in jail in nearby buildings, and Pere Antoine is often seen walking nearby. For a ghost hunter or paranormal researcher, this location would be the dream residence to live in, with access to

Is Andrew Jackson tipping his hat to the baroness, or his mistress in one of the apartments? You decide.

observe paranormal activity 24 hours a day. Almost every chapter in this book has some connection to this area, and many of the ghosts in the city once walked this area while alive.

Andrew Jackson is memorialized in Jackson Square with his statue. The statue of Jackson on his horse depicts him tipping his hat in the air, pointing toward one of the Pontalba Apartments. The legends stating why his hat is tipped in this direction are as vast as the ghost stories in New Orleans. Some say that he is tipping his hat in regards to the Baroness Pontalba, who donated a large sum of money to have the statue commissioned. Others say that Jackson did not care for the baroness, and that she only agreed to donate the money for the statue if it were depicting him eternally tipping his hat to her. I cannot confirm either story; it may be as simple as the artist's depiction of Jackson as a friendly representation, with him tipping his hat to all of New Orleans. I have heard a wide variety of stories regarding the statue, and some tour guides shared the legend with me that Jackson is actually tipping his hat to a certain apartment there in the Pontalba building where his mistress lived.

This mystery, like many others in New Orleans, continues to delight and entertain all who visit the city. This truly is part of the magic of New Orleans, as the joie de vivre ("cheerful enjoyment of life and exultation of spirit") is evident in the music, magic, and ghostly mayhem through the streets and is as beloved today by the living and the dead as it has been for hundreds of years.

 KALA'S TRAVEL TIPS

It's been my pleasure to be your travel guide to the other side during this journey through the haunted history and legends of New Orleans. I hope that you'll visit the city soon and enjoy the spirit and spirits that the city has to offer. Here are a few last tips that you may enjoy during your time in the city:

- **Almonaster Road** in New Orleans was named after Don Andres in honor and appreciation of his contributions to the city.
- The baroness left such a mark on the city that an opera was named after her titled **Pontalba: A Louisiana Legacy.**

Consider creating a bucket list of things you'd like to do in New Orleans from the travel tips here in the book including:

- **Wear Carnival beads** and maybe a boa while walking down Bourbon Street with a yard-long daiquiri cup in hand.
- Buy something with the **fleur-de-lis emblem** to remind you of the historic French roots of the city.
- Visit a **city of the dead,** and then light a candle in the world-famous St. Louis Cathedral in honor of all those who once lived in New Orleans.

- Activate your mojo and visit a **Voodoo shop** in the French Quarter.
- Make a list of all the **restaurants** you can try while in the city, making sure to eat red beans and rice, jambalaya, a po'boy, and, of course, some gumbo!
- Support a **local musician and artist** while in the city, pick up a painting you love from a local gallery or even off the street in front of Jackson Square, and/or buy a CD from a musician playing along the streets in the quarter.
- Go shopping in all the wonderful stores throughout the city. One of my favorite stores in the French Quarter to buy souvenirs, including a large handmade gator head by a local artist, is at the **New Orleans To Go** shop on the corner of Toulouse and Royal Streets.
- Take a **Mississippi riverboat cruise** and see New Orleans from the water, just like many traders and sailors once did.
- Get covered in powdered sugar while eating **beignets at Café du Monde,** and then go shopping in the nearby **French Market.**
- Ride the **streetcars** like Tennessee Williams and thousands of others have.
- And of course, go on a haunted **carriage ride** and tour the city to see the haunted places mentioned here in the book.

And don't forget your camera . . . *Happy Haunting!*

Visiting the Haunted Sites

Absinthe House
240 Bourbon Street
New Orleans, LA 70130
oldabsinthehouse.com

Andrew Jackson Hotel
919 Royal Street
New Orleans, LA 70116
frenchquarterinns.com/andrew
  jackson/location.html

Antoine's Restaurant
713 Rue Saint Louis
New Orleans, LA 70130
antoines.com

Arnaud's Restaurant
813 Rue Bienville
New Orleans, LA 70112
arnaudsrestaurant.com

Audubon Park and Zoo
6500 Magazine Street
New Orleans, LA 70118
auduboninstitute.org

Beauregard–Keyes House
1113 Chartres Street
New Orleans, LA 70116
bkhouse.org

Bottom of the Cup Tea Room
327 Chartres Street
New Orleans, LA 70130
bottomofthecup.com

Bourbon Orleans Hotel
717 Orleans Street
New Orleans, LA 70116
bourbonorleans.com

Brennan's Restaurant
417 Royal Street
New Orleans, LA 70130
brennansneworleans.com

Cabildo Museum
701 Chartres Street
Jackson Square
New Orleans, LA 70116
crt.state.la.us/museum

Café du Monde
800 Decatur Street
New Orleans, LA 70116
cafedumonde.com

Camellia Grill
626 S. Carrollton Avenue
New Orleans, LA 70094

Charity Hospital Cemetery
5050 Canal Street
New Orleans, LA 70179

Chevra Thilim Cemetery
4824 Canal Street
New Orleans, LA 70119

Commander's Palace Restaurant
1403 Washington Avenue
New Orleans, LA 70130
commanderspalace.com

Congo Square/Armstrong Park
835 N. Rampart Street
New Orleans, LA 70116

Cornstalk Hotel
915 Royal Street
New Orleans, LA 70116
cornstalkhotel.com

Court of Two Sisters Restaurant
613 Royal Street
New Orleans, LA 70130
courtoftwosisters.com

Cypress Grove Cemetery
120 City Park Avenue
New Orleans, LA 70124

Dauphine Orleans Hotel
415 Dauphine Street
New Orleans, LA 70112
dauphineorleans.com

Dispersed of Judah Cemetery
4937 Canal Street
New Orleans, LA 70119

Domilise Sandwich Shop
5240 Annunciation Street
New Orleans, LA 70115

Faulkner House Books
624 Pirate's Alley
New Orleans, LA 70119
faulknerhouse.net

French Market
1008 N. Peters Street
New Orleans, LA 70116
frenchmarket.org

Gallier House
1132 Royal Street
New Orleans, LA 70116
hgghh.org

Gardette–LePrete House
716 Dauphine Street
New Orleans, LA 70115

Gates of Prayer Cemetery
4824 Canal Street
New Orleans, LA 70124

Greenwood Cemetery
5242 Canal Boulevard
City Park Avenue at Canal Street
New Orleans, LA 70124

Holt Cemetery
635 City Park Avenue
New Orleans, LA 70119

Hotel Monteleone
214 Royal Street
New Orleans, LA 70130
hotelmonteleone.com

Inn on Bourbon Hotel
541 Bourbon Street
New Orleans, LA 70130
innonbourbon.com

Jackson Square
On Decatur Street, between the
    Jax Brewery Shopping Mall and
    the French Market, in front of
St. Louis Cathedral
New Orleans, LA 70116
jackson-square.com

Jacques-Imos Café
8324 Oak Street
New Orleans, LA 70118
jacquesimoscafe.com

Jazz Fest
nojazzfest.com

Lafayette Cemetery
1400 Washington Avenue
New Orleans, LA 70115

Lafitte's Blacksmith Shop Bar
941 Bourbon Street
New Orleans, LA 70116
lafittesblacksmithshop.com

LaLaurie House
1140 Royal Street
New Orleans, LA 70116

Louisiana State Museum
701 Chartres Street
Jackson Square
New Orleans, LA 70116
crt.state.la.us/museum

Loyola University
6363 St. Charles Avenue
New Orleans, LA 70118
loyno.edu

**Mahalia Jackson Theater for
    Performing Arts**
1419 Basin Street
New Orleans, LA 70116
mahaliajacksontheater.com

Mardi Gras World
1380 Port of New Orleans Place
New Orleans, LA 70130
mardigrasworld.com

Marie Laveau's House of Voodoo
739 Bourbon Street
New Orleans, LA 70116
voodooneworleans.com

Masonic Cemetery
400 City Park Avenue
New Orleans, LA 70122

Metairie Cemetery
5100 Pontchartrain Blvd
New Orleans, LA 70124

Napoleon House
500 Chartres Street
New Orleans, LA 70130
napoleonhouse.com

National Shrine of Our Lady of
  Prompt Succor
2701 State Street
New Orleans, LA 70118
shrineofourladyofpromptsuccor
  .com/About-Us.html

New Orleans Street Cars
norta.com

New Orleans To Go
601 Royal Street
New Orleans, LA 70130
neworleanstogo.com

New Orleans Voodoo Museum
724 Dumaine Street
New Orleans, LA 70116
voodoomuseum.com

Odd Fellows Rest Cemetery
5055 Canal Street
New Orleans, LA 70119

Our Lady of Guadalupe Church
411 N. Rampart Street
New Orleans, LA 70112
judeshrine.com

Pat O'Brien's
718 St. Peter Street
New Orleans, LA 70130
patobriens.com

Pere Antoine Alley
Next to Jackson Square
New Orleans, LA 70116

Pirates Alley
Next to Jackson Square
New Orleans, LA 70116

Place d'Armes Hotel
625 St. Ann Street
New Orleans, LA 70116
placedarmes.com

Pontalba Apartments
523 St. Ann Street and St. Peter
  Street
New Orleans, LA 70116
louisianatravel.com/louisiana-
  state-museum-1850-house

Port of New Orleans
1350 Port of New Orleans Place
New Orleans, LA 70123
portno.com

Reverend Zombie's House of
  Voodoo
725 St. Peter Street
New Orleans, LA 70116
voodooneworleans.com

Save Our Cemeteries
501 Basin Street, #3C
New Orleans, LA 70112
saveourcemeteries.org

St. Louis Cathedral
615 Pere Antoine Alley
New Orleans, LA 70116
stlouiscathedral.org

**St. John/Hope Mausoleum
  Cemetery**
4841 Canal Street
New Orleans, LA 70119

St. Louis Cemetery #1
Basin Street at St. Louis Street
New Orleans, LA 70119

St. Louis Cemetery #2
720 St. Louis Street
New Orleans, LA 70122

St. Louis Cemetery #3
3421 Esplanade Avenue
New Orleans, LA 70112

**St. Patrick Cemetery #1, #2,
  and #3**
143 City Park Avenue
New Orleans, LA 70119

Tipitana's
501 Napoleon Avenue
New Orleans, LA 70115
tipitinas.com

Toulouse Royale
601 Royal Street
New Orleans, LA 70130
neworleanstogo.com

Tulane University
6823 St. Charles Avenue
New Orleans, LA 70118
tulane.edu

Ursuline Convent
1100 Chartres Street
New Orleans, LA 70116
neworleansonline.com/directory/
  location.php?locationID=1278

WWOZ Radio
90.7 FM
wwoz.org

Yesteryears
626 Bourbon Street
New Orleans, LA 70130

Bibliography

Asbury, Herbert. *The French Quarter: An Informal History of the New Orleans Underworld*. New York: Basic Books, 1936.

Cable, George W. *The Creoles of Louisiana*. Gretna, LA: Pelican Publishing, 2005.

Cable, George W. *Strange True Stories of Louisiana*. Gretna, LA: Pelican Publishing, 1994.

Davis, Wade. *The Serpent and the Rainbow: A Harvard Scientist's Astonishing Journey into the Secret Societies of Haitian Voodoo, Zombies, and Magic*. New York: Simon & Schuster, 1997.

Davis, William C. *The Pirates Lafitte: The Treacherous World of the Corsairs of the Gulf*. Orlando, FL: Harcourt Press, 2005.

Filan, Kenaz. *The New Orleans Voodoo Handbook*. Rochester, VT: Inner Traditions, 2011.

Florence, Robert. *New Orleans Cemeteries: Life in the City of the Dead*. New Orleans: Batture Press, 1997.

Gehman, Mary. *Women and New Orleans: A History*. New Orleans: Margaret Media, 2004.

Gessler, Diana Hollingsworth. *Very New Orleans: A Celebration of History, Culture, and Cajun Country Charm*. Chapel Hill, NC: Algonquin Books, 2006.

Groom, Winston. *Patriotic Fire: Andrew Jackson and Jean Lafitte at the Battle of New Orleans*. Ann Arbor, MI: University of Michigan Press, 2006.

Long, Carolyn Morrow. *A New Orleans Voudou Priestess: The Legend and Reality of Marie Laveau*. Gainesville, FL: University Press of Florida, 2007.

Love, Victoria Cosner and Lorelei Shannon. *Mad Madame LaLaurie: New Orleans Most Famous Murderess Revealed*. Charleston, SC: The History Press, 2011.

Piazza, Tom. *Why New Orleans Matters*. New York: Harper Collins, 2005.

Rose, Al. *Storyville New Orleans: Being an Authentic, Illustrated Account of the Notorious Red-Light District*. Tuscaloosa, AL: University of Alabama Press, 1974.

Saxon, Lyle, Edward Dreyer, and Robert Tallant. *Gumbo Ya-Ya: Folk Tales of Louisiana*. Gretna, LA: Pelican Publishing, 2012.

Sublette, Ned. *The World That Made New Orleans: From Spanish Silver to Congo Square*. Chicago: Lawrence Hill Books, 2009.

Tallant, Robert. *Voodoo in New Orleans*. Gretna, LA: Pelican Publishing, 2012.

Taylor, Troy. *Haunted New Orleans: History and Hauntings of the Crescent City*. Charleston, SC: Haunted America, 2010.

About the Author

Kala Ambrose is a noted inspirational speaker, author, psychic, wisdom teacher, medium, and host of the *Explore Your Spirit with Kala* radio show (ExploreYourSpirit.com). Her teachings are described as discerning, empowering, and inspiring. Whether she's speaking with world-renowned experts on the *Explore Your Spirit with Kala* radio show, writing about empowering lifestyle choices, reporting on new discoveries in the scientific and spiritual arenas, or teaching groups around the country, fans around the world tune in daily for her inspirational musings and lively thought-provoking conversations.

Kala is the author of four books, including the award-winning *9 Life Altering Lessons: Secrets of the Mystery Schools Unveiled, Ghosthunting North Carolina, The Awakened Aura: Experiencing the Evolution of Your Energy Body,* and *Spirits of New Orleans: Voodoo Curses, Vampire Legends, and Cities of the Dead.*

A highly interactive psychic and wisdom teacher on a mission to educate, entertain, and inspire, Kala writes for *The Huffington Post* and presents workshops nationally on the mind/body/spirit connection, including auras and energy fields; business intuition; haunted history; and wisdom teachings at the Omega Institute, John Edward Presents Infinite Quest, the Learning Annex, Lily Dale Assembly, and DailyOM.

9 781578 605095